The Open University

Social Sciences: a second level course Urban development Units 30-33

The future city

Prepared by the Course Team

The Open University Press

The Open University Press
Walton Hall Milton Keynes

First published 1973

Designed by the Media Development Group of the Open University

Printed in Great Britain by
COES THE PRINTERS LIMITED
RUSTINGTON SUSSEX

ISBN 0 335 01747 9

This text forms part of an Open University course. The complete list of units in the course appears at the end of this text.

For general availability of supporting material referred to in this text, please write to the Director of Marketing, The Open University, P.O. Box 81, Walton Hall, Milton Keynes MK7 6AA.

Further information on Open University courses may be obtained from the Admissions Office, The Open University, P.O. Box 48, Walton Hall, Milton Keynes MK7 6AA.

1.1

Block 8 Units 30-33 Contents

DT201   Block 8 — Study Programme

Part of block	Set reading	Source of work	Graded reading
Unit 30	**1 The future urban society**	Course text	1
	2 P. Wilmott 'Some social trends'	Offprint	2
	3 P. A. Stone 'Resources and the economic framework'	Offprint	2
	4 J. S. Whyte 'The impact of telecommunications on town planning'	Offprint	2
	5 C. Jencks 'Philosophies of the future'	Offprint	2
Unit 31	**1 The future urban form**	Course text	1
	2 K. Lynch 'The pattern of the metropolis'	Offprint	2
	3 J. Friedmann, J. Miller 'The urban field'	Offprint	2
	4 L. March 'Homes beyond the fringe'	Offprint	2
	5 L. Martin 'The grid as generator'	Offprint	2
Unit 32	**1 Goals for urban development**	Course text	1
	2 R. Banham et al 'Non-plan; an experiment in freedom'	Offprint	2
	3 M. M. Webber 'Planning in an environment of change: permissive planning'	Offprint	2
	4 C. Alexander 'Major changes in environmental form required by social and psychological demands'	Offprint	2
Unit 33	**1 The demise of the city?**	Course text	1
	2 S. Greer 'The changing image of the city'	Offprint	2
	3 M. M. Webber 'The Post-city age' (in Bourne)	Set book	2
	4 The Ecologist 'Creating a new social system'	Offprint	2
	5 B. Ward, R. Dubos 'Human needs'	Offprint	2

Broadcast material for this block is listed separately in Audio-visual Handbook 4

KEY   1 Thorough reading leading to mastery of overall argument and method of analysis
        2 General reading to gain an acquaintance with overall argument

4

Introduction to Block 8   The future city

Webber (1968) has contrasted the conventional attitudes to the future of pre-industrial, industrial and post-industrial societies. In the former the future is either unknowable or influenced through the good offices of the local deity. In industrial societies the phenomena of compound interest, mortgages and insurance testify to an idea of the future as an extension of the present. The post-industrial view, held at the present time mainly by futurists and planners, but anticipated by Utopians in the past, is of a future which is to a considerable degree open and which may be radically different from the present. It is the latter view which is axiomatic in this block and the Reader which accompanies it.

The post-industrial view of the future differs from those of the past because it has been articulated into a fairly well-defined method. This involves thought in two modes – from present to future and from future to present. Projection of present trends (a method developed from the industrial view) allows one to forecast the probability of various future events. Critical study of projections allow one to isolate external factors affecting trends and to discern contradiction between trends, which will necessitate choices of priority at some future date. Early choices lead on to more choices and thus we find in the medium to long term a ramifying set of possible futures. The second mode of thought, from future to present, usually involves selecting particularly desirable or undesirable futures and then tracing them back to the present policy or action necessary to bring them about. The two directions of thought are often referred to as *exploratory* and *normative* forecasting respectively. Jantsch (1967) has suggested that these two modes should always be combined: extrapolations of the present will be altered if there is a change in values or goals and the most perfect goal becomes irrelevant if there is no practical route by which it can be reached from the present.

This model of future thinking points up some of the inadequacies of the more traditional utopian thinkers – and also some of their strengths. The major weakness in most utopias is that, although the future state of society is usually presented in detail, the process by which it came about is presented sketchily, if at all. There is rarely an attempt to assess its probability. The major strength of the utopian method is most plainly demonstrated in cases where the future society has been deliberately made unpleasant: here the authors are not concerned to chart how dystopian societies have evolved but are attempting to show graphically that they *might* come about. The intent is to motivate ordinary people to think about their future and to make them hostile to certain trends. The effectiveness of novels like *Brave New World* and *1984* in alerting the public to the seeds of totalitarianism in current society and technology highlights the failure of more recent futurists to communicate.

The question of communication raises an even more fundamental question: to whom does the future belong? Once goals for the distant future have been incorporated into the planning process, they begin to affect the very immediate future. If only a small group of intellectuals are deemed fit to discuss the distant future, the political process swings towards the anti-democratic pole. However, although the techniques of forecasting are rather esoteric, the choice of goals is open to everybody: a goal directed planning may thus be democratic whereas a means-centred planning moves society towards the centralized power structure of *Brave New World* and *1984*.

The block expands the post industrial model of the future described above. Units 30 and 31 are exploratory, investigating the constraints and trends which exist at present and which must be accommodated in any future. These involve resources, economics, geometry and social convention. Unit 32 adopts a normative stance and investigates the sort of goals at which we might aim. A survey of literary and design utopias and of the goals of the planning profession indicates some possibilities – but the implicit goals of business and commerce provide a strong contrast. Unit 33 examines the concept of increasing scale and considers whether the city will survive as a spatial form or distinctive social organization. The block concludes by questioning the future of society itself if present trends continue. These trends are a major theme of the Reader, in which we have tried to err, if at all, on the side of pessimism. We hope that this confrontation with the future may lead you to question whether it is appropriate to your own goals and, if not, to induce you to take action to modify it.

Aims

The main aims of this block are:
1 To summarize the course through the adoption of a future perspective.
2 To identify the major social, economic, technological, and political trends that will shape the city of the future (Unit 30).
3 To explore the alternative forms of the future city (Unit 31).
4 To examine the potential goals of urban development and to encourage the making of deliberate choices among them (Unit 32).
5 To speculate on the future role and relevance of the city in the society of the future (Unit 33).
Four of these aims relate to specific units but they should be seen as an integrated whole rather than as separate entities.

As stated above, the future perspective we have adopted emphasizes a dialectical integration between forecasting future trends and devising policies to reach stated goals. Both forecasting and policy formulation draw our attention to the fact that the many subsystems which have been analysed in this course are inextricably linked into a city-system which is in turn only a subsystem of society at large. This block on the future of the city thus involves academic synthesis of foregoing material as well as discussions of policies and likelihoods for the future.

Form and teaching function of the block

As usual, the correspondence text provides the backbone of the argument of the block. In addition we are asking you to read a number of excerpts in the special Block Reader which has been edited by the unit authors. Detailed reading instructions are included in each unit. Your active participation is encouraged by the liberal use of self-assessment questions. Finally, we must add that, although the block has no continuous assessment, it will be given a greater weight in the final examination than other blocks.

References

JANTSCH, E. (1967) *Technological forecasting in perspective*, Paris, Organization for Economic Cooperation and Development.

WEBBER, M. (1968) 'Planning in an environment of change: beyond the industrial age' in *Town Planning Review*, 39, 3, pp 179–95.

Unit 30 The future urban society
Andrew Blowers and Chris Hamnett

Part cover: Collage based on the Habitat formula
Source: *Civilia*, a proposed New Town, edited by Ivor de Wolfe, The Architectural Press

Contents Unit 30

1 Aims, objectives and reading guide

Aims

The main aims of this unit are:

1 to describe the human and physical factors that operate as constraints upon the choice between alternative courses of urban development;

2 to identify the major trends in urban society that are likely to influence development until about the year 2000;

3 to discuss the possible alternative courses of urban development and to encourage awareness of the choices available.

We shall attempt to fulfil these aims by:

a reference to current trends in urban development that have been discussed in other parts of the course and which can be projected into the future;

b integration of this unit with selected readings (reproduced in the Reader) on the determinants and constraints of future development;

c discussion in this unit of the potential economic, social and technological changes that are likely to influence the nature of urban development in the western world.

In this way the unit should provide a background to the more specific issues raised in other parts of the block, and in the Reader.

Objectives

After reading this unit and the associated excerpts in the Reader you should be able to:

1 understand what is meant by future and its relevance to the process of urban development;

2 comprehend the terms *primary* and *secondary* forecasting and evaluate them as methods of predicting the future;

3 distinguish between *inexorable* and *inevitable* trends;

4 recognize and describe the major environmental constraints upon future urban development;

5 identify the major demographic, economic, social and technological changes that are likely to shape the future urban society.

Objective 5 may help you to prepare for Unit 31 in that you should be able to indicate the probable influence of rising income levels, income differentials, changing work patterns and changes in personal transport and communications technology on the spatial structure and pattern of future urban forms.

Finally, you might also like to speculate on two related issues which arise from the underlying assumptions of the unit itself.

a How far can the constraints and trends discussed here be applied to future urban development in the developing countries and in the communist world?

b How far are the trends discussed here capable of general application at all levels of society within the western capitalist world?

You should be able to reach some conclusions on these issues on the basis of the correspondence texts and the Media components you have been studying so far.

Reading guide

There are four articles reproduced in the Reader which are *required* reading for this unit. They are:

1 WILLMOTT, P. (1969) 'Some social trends' in Cowan, P. (ed) (1969) 'Developing patterns of urbanization', *Urban Studies*, 6, 3.
This article gives a broad perspective of the ways in which the social structure and the patterns of social life in Britain are likely to develop over the next twenty to thirty years. Among the trends it covers are the potential changes in

occupational structure and economic growth, family size and income patterns, leisure, mobility and the settlement pattern.

2 STONE, P. A. (1969) 'Resources and the economic framework' in Cowan, P. (ed) (1969) 'Developing patterns of urbanization', *Urban Studies*, 6, 3.
Stone's paper covers much of the same ground as Willmott's but it emphasizes the constraints on the future. It is especially relevant to Section 4 of the unit on the environmental constraints.

3 WHYTE, J. S. (1970) *The impact of telecommunications on town planning*, Town and Country Planning Summer School, Swansea, 1970, pp 27–30.
Whyte's paper discusses the historical background to developments in telecommunications and their influence upon town planning. He indicates the potential developments of the future, how they might be utilized, and what their spatial implications might be. You should read this as background to Sections 5.3.3 to 5.3.5.

4 JENCKS, C. (1971) 'Philosophies of the future', in *Architecture 2000*, London, Studio Vista, pp 20–32.
Jencks makes the important distinction between inevitable and inexorable trends. He condemns the attitude of compliance to an inevitable fate adopted by the 'weak determinists'. There is considerable freedom to decide the course of the future. You should read this in conjunction with Sections 2 and 3 of the unit.

There are five extracts that we *recommend* you to read with this unit. They are:

1 TOFFLER, M. (1973) Excerpt from *Future Shock*, Pan Books.
Future Shock is 'the shattering stress and disorientation that we induce in individuals by subjecting them to too much change in too short a time'. Toffler's book dramatically portrays a great many of the contemporary trends that may well have a large influence on our future. The extract examines the loss of our 'sense of place' consequent upon heightened mobility.

2 BUCHANAN, C. (1964) 'The future of the motor vehicle' in *Traffic in Towns*, Penguin Books, pp 31–43.
This is part of a very influential report which investigated the future growth of motor traffic and the action that would be necessary to accommodate it without excessive damage to the built environment. Here the impact of the increase in car ownership on the future form of British cities is examined. This piece is relevant to Section 5.3.2 of the unit.

3 TILLINGHAST, P. (1968) 'Leisure: old patterns and new problems' in Anderson, S. (ed) (1968) *Planning for diversity and choice*, MIT Press, pp 143–53.
Tillinghast defines leisure as 'anything not done for the sake of something else but for its own sake'. He suggests that the employment of leisure time in the future will create a major social challenge and require a complete reorientation of our work dominated society. Read this in connection with Section 5.2.

4 The Ecologist (1972) 'Creating a new social system' in *A Blueprint for Survival*, first published in *The Ecologist* 2, 1; Revised edition published by Penguin Books, 1972. (Reproduced in the Reader.)
This extract is required reading for Unit 33. It may also be read in conjunction with Section 4.2 of this unit, for it examines the nature of the new social system that may result from increasing decentralization.

5 MEIER, R. (1969) 'Material resources' in Jungk, R. and Galtung, J. (1969) *Mankind 2000*, Allen and Unwin.
Meier discusses the resources and technology on the future development of cities in the developing countries. Looking at the growing scarcity of physical

resources, he advocates the rapid substitution of non physical resources, in particular knowledge and information, and describes the possible effects on both society and the city. This is relevant to Section 4.3 of the unit.

2 Anticipating the future

... The future depends upon the present, and the present ... depends upon the past and the past is unalterable. (Samuel Butler, *Erewhon*)

There are few people, we would imagine, who would dispute the interrelationship of the present and the immediate future in our lives – be it looking forward to the next meal or planning how to spend the next pay packet. As Charles Jencks puts it:

... Anticipating the future is as unavoidable and commonplace as breathing. Perhaps like breathing it is also involuntary and mechanical. When we follow the flight of a bird we anticipate its future course and position; we reach out to catch a falling object; we pull back to avoid an impending blow. (Jencks 1971 p 9)

Contemplation of the more distant future is equally inescapable and ranges from fatalism to intense concern. In western societies concern about the future seems to be growing. One reason for this is the increasing complexity of society. 'One of the striking features of the biological world, in all its diversity, is that the perpetuation of a species becomes a more and more intricate problem the higher the species ranks on the ladder of beings' (de Jouvenel 1967 p 7). This growing concern for the future is a relatively recent development and it has also been stimulated by a second trend in western society, the increasing pace of change. Until recently the future could hardly be said to comprise a distinct problem in any shape or form, largely because of its essential similarity to both past and present. C. P. Snow has outlined why this was so: 'Until this century social change was so slow that it could pass unnoticed in one person's lifetime. That is no longer so. The rate of change has increased so much that our imagination can't keep up' (Snow 1959 p 12).

It is the rate of change, both social and technical that is so crucial, and which has led Alvin Toffler (1970) to coin the phrase 'The Death of Permanence'. Think of the changes that have occurred during the last two decades in British cities. Increasing car ownership has brought about a reorganization of work journeys, shopping and leisure habits. Changes in the employment structure have increased the employment opportunities in service industries while those in heavy industries have been reduced. This has been reflected in a concentration of office work in city centres whereas manufacturing industries have tended to move out or grow in the suburbs (Unit 13). A regional redistribution of employment opportunities has also occurred with growth tending to be most rapid in the southern parts of the UK while in some parts of the older industrial areas there is evidence of a decline in activity. These and other processes have visibly altered our cities and have reacted upon urban society. The impact of new forms of telecommunication is now being felt (Unit 18). Change is occurring at an increasingly rapid rate and the corollary of this is that the future is likely to be increasingly different from the present, let alone the past.

These two complementary trends – the increasing complexity of society and the accelerating pace of change have encouraged individuals and society as a whole not merely to anticipate the future but, wherever possible and desirable, to influence its outcome. We not only think about the future, we deliberately plan its achievement.

In planning for the future urban society we must recognize the intimate relationship between past, present and future. Just as the future exerts an influence on the present, so too the present and the past act as constraints upon the future. The most obvious constraints are the environmental ones. Much of the existing physical fabric of our cities will be standing in the next century. The limitations of space and resources that the environment imposes on future development have become a major source of concern (Unit 33). The constraints on the future urban society are a major theme of this unit.

Constraints modify but do not determine the course of development. The future is, in large measure, the product of human action or inaction. The main purpose of this block is to show that we are confronted with alternative futures and that we have the power to choose among them. In addition to a succession of *probable* futures every society faces an array of *possible* futures, and a conflict over *preferable* ones. 'The management of change is the effort to convert certain possibles into probables, in pursuit of agreed preferables. Determining the probable calls for a science of futurism. Delineating the possible calls for an art of futurism. Defining the preferable calls for a politics of futurism' (Toffler 1970 p 407). The task of futurism is twofold. First, it must decide which future is most probable and ask whether or not we want it. (This is the primary concern of this unit.) Second, it asks which possible future we prefer and attempts to provide a programme to achieve it. (This is what Unit 32 sets out to do.) The first function is more concerned with forecasting, the second with goal setting.

3 Forecasting

It should not be assumed from the foregoing that we can predict the future in any scientific sense. As de Jouvenel has pointed out, knowledge of the future is a contradiction in terms for we can only have positive knowledge of the past and present. Hypotheses about the future are not capable of empirical verification until it becomes the present. Thus, de Jouvenel asserts that when we speak of 'a forecast' we simply mean a carefully formed opinion about the future. In consequence de Jouvenel rejects the possibility of a 'science of the future' in favour of the art of 'reasoned conjecture'.

> ... The reason why the word 'conjecture' ... (is used) ... is precisely that it is opposed to the term 'knowledge' ... The intellectual construction of a likely future is a work of art ... In this 'composition' of the mind, we should make use of all the relevant causal connections we can find ... What is of vital importance for the progress of this art of conjecture is that an assertion about the future should be accompanied by the intellectual scaffolding which supports it, and should be subject to criticism. (de Jouvenel 1967 p 17)

de Jouvenel divides forecasts into two basic types – *primary* and *secondary* forecasts. A primary forecast is termed such 'not because it is a fairly simple intellectual procedure, but because it represents a first stage in our dealing with the future course of a phenomenon' (de Jouvenel 1967 p 53). In other words a primary forecast states that X is likely to happen unless other action is taken. A secondary forecast, on the other hand, represents what is likely to happen *if* the certain action is taken. Indeed, as de Jouvenel points out 'The primary forecast is not an inevitable course of things ... our motive in formulating it is to provoke action apt to change it'[1] (de Jouvenel 1967 p 53).

de Jouvenel distinguishes at least eight modes of primary prediction in his work *The Art of Conjecture*, among the more important of which are extrapolation, analogy, signalling, and causality. Taking these in turn, *extrapolation* is without

---

1 This classification is similar to Jantsch's *exploratory* and *normative* forecasts referred to in the block introduction.

doubt the most common type of forecasting as well as being the most intellectually dubious. Here 'the supposition is that the future will differ from the present in the same way as the present differs from the past' (Young 1968 p 13). de Jouvenel summed up its major weakness when he wrote 'The trouble with prolongation of a tendency is that the reversal of the tendency is not anticipated' (de Jouvenel 1967 p 63). In reality there are frequent cyclical movements and reversals. Jencks (see Reader) compares society to an 'open system', one characteristic of which is a tendency to become unbalanced. But, as Jencks notes 'all trends do not continue indefinitely; they always reach a point of equilibrium either because counteraction is taken, because the environment is saturated or because of a counter-trend' (Jencks 1971, p 27). One common example is that of birth rates (see Willmott and Stone in Reader).

If the settled human population had always had a natural increase (ie excess of births over deaths) of one per cent per year we would by now have 'a sphere of living flesh, many thousands of light years in diameter, expanding at a radial velocity many times faster than the speed of light' (Goldsmith 1971 pp 208–9). In fact there has been a tendency for birth and death rates to move in sympathy with each other although there is often a considerable time lag before the adjustment is made. In western societies it is probable that among the reasons for currently declining birth rates is the fear of overpopulation.

Forecasting by *analogy*, or the classification of situations on the basis of their similarities is, according to de Jouvenel, more rational than extrapolation.

. . . To anticipate by extrapolation is to take things as they come – the intellectual effort involved is minimal, whereas a prediction by analogy presupposes that the mind has sufficiently delineated the present situation to find some analogues for it, judging the resemblance to be fundamental enough for the same sort of events to follow as in the reference situation . . .

In asking whether the resemblance is sufficient, we raise the question of determining factors. Unless two situations resemble each other in respects that are causally significant, we can hardly expect the same effects to follow. (de Jouvenel 1967 p 65)

By way of example we can take the forecast that segregation of age groups within cities will occur, just as segregation by social class exists. In both cases, it may be argued, the determining factor is that people with similar demographic and social characteristics tend to group together.

Signalling or, as de Jouvenel terms it 'the Railway', may be described as one sequence of events conforming to an earlier one, and being 'signalled' by them. The different sequences of events being like trains travelling some distance behind one another on the same track. Two examples of this type of forecasting are those forecasts concerning the future of the 'developing nations' – usually conceived as being on the western capitalist track, and the growth of car ownership and an auto-based culture in western Europe along the lines of North America. de Jouvenel believes that this type of forecast has so little foundation in reason that it would not deserve to be mentioned were it not for the fact that it frequently functions as a hidden assumption in a forecast.

Finally, there is *causality*, which de Jouvenel defines as the discovery of a cause which will continue to act, and the specification of its necessary effect. An example of this could be that increases in crime and other types of social pathology are caused by the growth of cities. The evidence for this is the correlation between crime rates and city size. Unfortunately, as de Jouvenel notes 'This is a method of prediction based on a very sound principle. But its practical application can be badly defective . . . causal relations in the social order lack simplicity and clarity' (de Jouvenel 1967 pp 67 and 71).

There are other modes of prediction which are defective in greater or lesser degree. There is no need to outline these, however, for you should have realized by now that forecasting is a notoriously difficult business, the difficulty of which increases with the length of time involved. It is comparatively easy for an individual to plan a day, a week, or even a month ahead and engagement diaries represent his organization of future time. Beyond this immediate future entries become sparse and the future more uncertain. In terms of space, too, we tend to be more concerned with events at the family and local scale rather than at a national or global scale (see Figure 1). Some flows are recurrent or cyclical in nature such as transport flows affecting the journey to work or shops, or to visit friends and relatives, or the flows of electronic communications. Some needs, such as education, health, housing and recreation are, in part, determined by population, size and structure and the availability of resources. These flows and needs can, within the limitations of resources, be anticipated and provided for. They are what de Jouvenel terms *structural certainties*.

Figure 1 Thinking of the future The space-time graph shows the relative importance of different time and space horizons in our thinking about the future. Most of us when thinking of the future tend to confine ourselves to immediate local events (see bottom left of diagram). More rarely do we focus on national or global long-term issues Source: *The Limits to Growth*, Earth Island Ltd, p 19

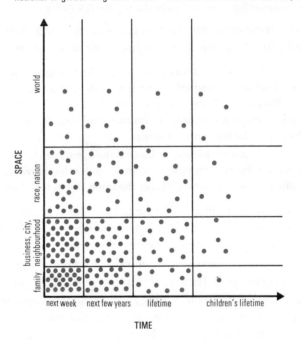

Over a longer term, however, the demand for services will change. The flows of people and of information will also alter in nature, frequency and intensity. In the still longer term the introduction of new economic, social, and technological determinants will bring about radical changes. These will also change the spatial scale for which decisions must be taken (Unit 31). de Jouvenel conceives of society as 'nothing but the contour or outline of a host of moving bodies' which is stable to the extent that the same repetitive patterns and mutual relations are maintained. To the extent that these are not 'episodic and periodic, deformations of the social surface can occur' which destroy our structural certainties. The task and problem of forecasting is, as de Jouvenel puts it, 'to apprehend, at their origin, those shoots which as they grow will deform the familiar social surface and produce swellings, fractures and cracks' (de Jouvenel 1967 p 39). Most of our comments up till now have implicitly assumed that things will go on as they are without conscious and

16

deliberate intervention. In this unit we shall be primarily concerned with primary forecasts of the urban future. There are also *secondary* forecasts which take into account the influence of planning. The prime purpose of planning however, is to change the future to a greater or lesser extent in specified directions. As such the influence of deliberate planning upon the future is potentially profound. Indeed, urban society, like individual lives, cannot be planned to forestall the unexpected or to secure vague goals for which the means of attainment are unspecified. Thus, goals for future urban development are the subject of Unit 32.

SAQ 1   What is the difference between primary and secondary forecasts?

SAQ 2   Here are four primary predictions concerning Calcutta. Indicate which of the four modes of primary predictions outlined in the text applies in each case:
a The future development of Calcutta will follow on similar lines to the past growth of London.
b The future development of Calcutta will represent an extension of the established pattern.
c The future development of Calcutta will depend upon its growth rate.
d The future development of Calcutta will be similar to that of Bombay.

4 The environmental constraints on the city of the future

Although the future is ours to choose, our range of choice will be circumscribed. Many of the constraints will be societal and can be overcome or, at least, modified by human action. There are also the absolute constraints imposed by the physical environment. These are land and natural resources.

4.1 Land

Although it can be argued that few parts of the world are overpopulated,[1] it is nevertheless conceivable that many parts of the world are becoming overcrowded. The competing demands for space are most intense in the highly urbanized parts of the earth. Here demands for housing, industrial, agricultural and recreational land have to be reconciled. Very often a system of allocation based upon market signals alone has 'led to types of land use that grossly contradicts amenity and human values' (Ward and Dubos in Reader). Recognition of this has led to tighter controls over land use planning.

Such controls have important urban consequences. They tend to encourage a more intensive use of land. There has been in western Europe, where controls have been invoked, an opportunity for cities to capitalize on their heritage by maintaining distinctive, dense urban forms (Hall 1968b). Growth is channelled in particular directions and, in some cases, related to freestanding satellites. In south east England, for example, the metropolitan Green Belt (Figure 2) effectively limits the expansion of London's continuously built-up area. Growth has been channelled into new towns by the government or has occurred spontaneously usually through private developers in many of the towns in the region. Green belts are, however, a man-made constraint and they were formulated as much for reasons of landscape aesthetics as for the conservation of agricultural land. Much more important is the growth of urban areas relative to the diminution of agricultural land.

[1] This is a controversial issue which we cannot deal with here. It is often contended that there is a fundamental world problem of overpopulation. It is arguable that the world does not suffer from problems of overpopulation *per se*, rather from a maldistribution of resources. More recently the interconnection of biological and natural systems has been stressed and the dangers of upsetting the ecological balance have been demonstrated (Unit 33).

Figure 2 London's 'Green Belt' Source: *Greater London*, Coppock & Prince, Faber, p 299

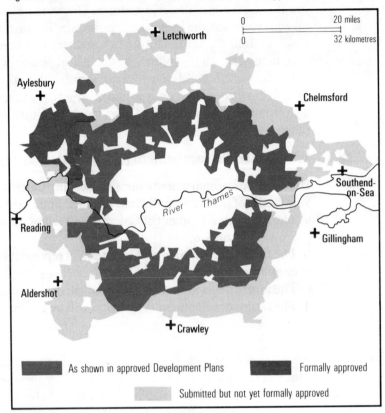

Since the development of new modes of urban transportation, such as the train, tube and car, towards the end of the nineteenth century, the urban acreage of England and Wales has approximately doubled from two million acres or five per cent of the total land area in 1900, to four million acres or ten per cent in 1960. Best (1965) has calculated that between 1927 and 1961 1,750,000 acres of farmland were lost to other uses, an average loss of 54,000 acres a year in England and Wales. The rate of loss has varied markedly, however, and was much greater before the Second World War than after it. Between 1950 and 1960 it was running at about 36,000 acres per year.

There are a variety of factors operating on land consumption. Of these, as Hall notes, 'the most fundamental of all is the rise in population' (Hall 1968a p 104, see Section 4.2 and Stone 1969 in Reader). Associated with it has been a rapid increase in *per capita* disposable income which is likely to continue into the foreseeable future leading to a doubling or trebling of real income *per capita* by the year 2000 (Webber 1963). One of the results of this will be an increase in car ownership and consequent demands for road and parking space. In Britain the number of cars is projected to rise from twelve million (1970) to nineteen million (1980) and thirty million (2000) (see Buchanan 1963 in Reader). Other developments such as increased leisure will add to the demands for more space. The implication of these trends is that overall densities are likely to decline during the remainder of this century. Best (1964) has calculated that on current trends the urban acreage of England and Wales could grow from four to five million acres by 1980, and to six million acres by the year 2000. In percentage terms this would represent a shift from just under eleven per cent (1960) to just over thirteen per cent (1980) to sixteen per cent (2000) of the total surface area – three times the urban acreage of 1900.

These are but overall figures, however, and in certain regions, notably the south-east of England, around London, the problem is much more marked. Best showed in his analysis that the percentage rate of urban growth over the decade 1950–60 tended to be greatest in the regions which were already most heavily urbanized. In the ring between fifteen and forty miles from central London, the rate of urbanization was more than double the national average. Thus, if present trends continue, by the year 2000 there will only be four acres of undeveloped land to every acre of developed land compared to a ratio of 8:1 in 1961. Within two hundred years the whole region will be developed. But the 'problem region' is the north west which, apart from its National Parks and land over 800 feet, will be completely developed for housing, factories, roads, airports, reservoirs, etc. by the year 2000 if present trends continue (*Guardian*, 25 April 1973).

Land for urban development must compete against other uses. Agricultural productivity has, up till now, more than made up for any losses of agricultural land in Britain. But domestic production only accounted for half the total food consumption. The demand for recreational land is certain to increase and the competition between these various uses will inevitably be most severe in those areas that are already heavily developed. England and Wales with an average population density of 324 per square mile (among the highest in the world apart from small island states like Hong Kong) is already experiencing problems of land shortage that will be encountered elsewhere if present trends continue.

4.2 Resource constraints

Resource constraints may be classified into two types. On the one hand there are the world wide resource constraints imposed by the finite natural resources and the stability of the world ecosystem (Unit 33). These may seem a far cry from the question of the future society, but without them we are unlikely to have a future. The depletion of certain minerals will lead to high prices and substitution, and, in some cases, to exhaustion. The intensive application of fertilisers and pesticides and the extensive use of monocultural practices may be short term benefits at the expense of a long term decline in fertility.[1] So, too, there is the whole question of effluent and waste disposal dealt with in Unit 16. There is a limit to the amount of atmospheric and marine pollution that the environment can support before serious deterioration in the quality of life sets in.

So far we have referred to the world wide resource constraints. There are also the more localized constraints – water for example. In Britain we are currently consuming some 25,000 million gallons a day, almost all from surface water which is directly related to rainfall. This source currently provides about 40,000 million gallons a day and is unlikely to be increased. If, as Emrys Jones suggests, 'we think in terms of the steadily increasing use of water, the margin begins to look precarious long before AD 2000' (Jones 1969 p 337). In Britain water is most plentiful where population density is at its lowest, ie on the upland areas to the north and west, and Birmingham, Liverpool and Manchester among our major cities are all having to pipe water from upland reservoirs, and plans for barrages on parts of the coast (Morecambe Bay, the Dee Estuary, and the Wash) have been put forward. In America, the water shortage in Los Angeles is so acute that it has to pipe water from the Colorado River.

---

[1] The evidence is conflicting though not necessarily contradictory. It depends on how you interpret it (see extract from 'Only One Earth' in the Reader).

4.3 The built environment 'Most world cities are prisoners of history' (Hall 1966 p 241). Although man-made, the built environment will act as a constraint on the city of the future since much of it will be standing well into the next century (see Stone 1969a in Reader). As Emrys Jones has commented: 'Although technology and society are dynamic, the environmental base is relatively fixed' (Jones 1969 p 335). The broad distribution of urban population has changed but little over the last century, and as we do not start with a clean slate, new patterns and developments can only be modifications of the old. Changes over the next thirty years are therefore unlikely to be wholly revolutionary, a fact which is likely to be reinforced by the slowly changing socio-psychological evaluations of the physical framework. Preferences and beliefs which are culturally based do not change overnight. In addition, none of us possesses freedom of choice over our environment. We are all constrained to some degree.

The changes in the built environment will also be uneven in geographical distribution. Although by the year 2000 the population and economic activity of Britain is likely to remain concentrated in a wide belt stretching from north west to south east England with outliers of dense population in central Scotland, north east England, and south Wales, the relative economic importance of the south is likely, if present trends continue, to increase further.

Since many modern industries are rarely fastidious in their locational needs but are rather 'footloose', they may be increasingly attracted to areas which can combine access to labour and markets with good amenity. This could mean increasing growth on the south coast of England, for example, or in a European context, in areas such as southern France. In the United States, California and Florida have proved attractive locations on amenity grounds. Meanwhile, the older industrial areas may continue to experience a relative decline. In some areas an absolute decline of economic activity and of population has already set in with profound consequences for the settlement pattern.

Change in the built environment will be slow especially in areas like Britain where population growth and urbanization have long passed their peak. Here a larger proportion of the new investment will be for replacement of the existing stock. The quality of the built environment of the future is, ultimately, an allocational question. Ortrude White puts it rather dramatically when she states that if one-third of the increase in GNP by 2000 were 'devoted to changing the physical environment, it would be enough to completely reconstruct a major conurbation such as Manchester or the west Midlands every year' (White 1969 p 10). She qualifies this by stating that 'it would be a foolish allocation of resources unless it can be shown . . . that an improved physical environment would result in an improvement in the quality of life proportional to such an expenditure'.

Changes in the built environment in Britain and many other advanced countries will be modest when compared to those likely in the developing world. At present about two-thirds of the population in the developing world are dependent upon agriculture. The process of urbanization is being experienced but its conditions are different from those that were experienced in the advanced countries. Urbanization has proceeded faster than industrialization and urban growth may be related to conditions in the rural hinterland and the high expectations that some groups have of the benefits of urban life (Unit 3). Meier regards urban development as the key to progress in the developing countries (Meier in Reader). But it should not follow the advanced western model which is profligate in its waste of resources. Instead 'the design of environments should reinforce resource conserving life-styles, holding consumption close to the minimum adequate standard, and taking advantage of economies of scale' (Meier 1969 p 103).

Since technology is improving the means of communication whereas the marginal costs of natural resources are bound to increase, cities of the future should substitute information and communication for scarce resources. A mixture of high technology industries and labour-intensive activities will maximize the development potential of expanding cities which will absorb the surplus population. Meier describes the process by which migrants will be absorbed into productive activity within the urban system. Finally, he outlines the physical appearance of these cities. In many respects they will be similar to present cities with a teeming, varied central area, and closely packed residential neighbourhoods achieving densities of 100,000 persons per square mile. Certain features will be absent, notably private vehicles. 'Urban transport is the most capital consuming utility, and its improvement requires the most careful planning. Any significant population of automobiles cannot be tolerated within resource conserving urbanism' (Meier 1969 p 111). Whatever pattern of urbanization emerges in these countries the existing built environment is likely to be a less significant constraint on the future city than will be the case in the highly urbanized developed countries.

5 The direction of change

So far we have emphasized the problems of forecasting and the constraints on the future – but what will the future be like? This depends on the direction of the changes experienced by urban society, and they are many, various and often conflicting. Of these future demographic, economic and technological changes are easier to forecast than the much more complex social changes. None can be predicted with any certainty and the further ahead we look the more general and unreliable our predictions become. It is our purpose here to indicate the probable trends of change in western urban society and the changes that might occur through the exercise of human choice.

5.1 Changes in the demographic structure

In a country like Britain where birth and death rates are low, any profound change in the population structure thirty years hence is unlikely. For one thing, the number of people over 30 at that time cannot be affected by changes in births (and shifts in the migration and death rates are likely to have only marginal impact on the accuracy of current predictions). But it is birth rates that are most volatile and which make projections of future population so difficult (Willmott and Stone in Reader). Postwar fluctuations in the birth rate have been reflected in considerable differences in forward projections (see Figure 1 in Stone in Reader).

In the 1930s and 1940s a nearly stable population was assumed. Then, in the 1950s and 1960s quite marked rises were forecast. The forecast for 2001 made in 1964 was 75 millions. However, the most recent forecast based on the 1971 Census lowered the estimates quite considerably to 66.5 millions, and it has since declined still further to 63.1 millions (see Figure 2 in Stone in Reader).

If birth rates remain relatively low up to the year 2000 the population will become 'older' (ie the proportion of people in the older age groups will increase). Conversely, higher birth rates will increase the proportion of younger dependents. In either case a decline in the proportion of the population of working age is likely with a concomitant increase in the dependency ratio (the proportion of the inactive to the active population). This has obvious planning implications, for if there is to be a youthful population the pressure will be on educational facilities, if an older population the emphasis will be on welfare.

The dependency ratio will also be increased through earlier retirement and a longer period in full-time education. Indeed, this may become a necessity, as a means of coping with the effects of growing automation and increasing leisure.

SAQ 3   What influence can individuals have on the growth and structure of population?

5.2 The future of work and leisure

Increased productivity through automation may have a number of effects. First, it may lead to higher unemployment. Second, there is likely to be a shift in employment structure from manual to non-manual occupations, a trend already advanced in the western world. Third, in the longer term there may be a considerable increase in leisure time. Whether this will be achieved through a shorter working day, or week, or increased holidays, will obviously vary as will the implications. It will also occur at a different pace between different economic activities and in different countries depending on the economic and social priorities that are set. How a reduction in working hours will be used is clearly a matter of individual choice. One British study showed that the marked fall in the number of hours in the standard working week (47.5 to 42) since the end of the Second World War had been exactly compensated for by an increase in the amount of overtime worked. This would seem to indicate that currently at least the average British worker opts for more money rather than more leisure when the choice presents itself. It is very possible, however, that greater affluence in the future will weigh the scales more towards leisure.

Assuming the trend does become a reality it may bring about a re-orientation of the work dominated society in advanced western countries. 'The ideologies that surround work and give it justification and value in individual and social terms may become strengthened in support of what remains of work and on the other hand they may increasingly come into doubt and become the objects of reaction and rebellion' (Kahn and Wiener 1967 p 194). For some people work will remain as a major drive but society may well confront what, according to Keynes, will be man's real problem, 'how to occupy his leisure which science and compound interest have won for him to live wisely and agreeably and well.' Kahn and Wiener point out the difficulties of adjustment in a society whose goals have been orientated towards acquisition and competition, where work has become regarded as the 'primary touch with reality' (Kahn and Wiener 1967 p 215).

Education is seen by many as the most hopeful means to achieve the adjustment to new goals, education for self improvement and fulfilment rather than for narrowly vocational ends.[1] Without doubt a considerable effort will be required to overcome the pervasive influence of the Protestant ethic, and adjust towards a more leisure-orientated society (Tillinghast in Reader). Assuming, of course, that that is what we want. It would be perhaps foolish to rid ourselves of work entirely, given that many thinkers regard it as a central necessity for our self-fulfilment.

1 The importance of education is stressed time and time again in the utopian literature (see Plato, More, Owen, etc). But this view is not unanimous and a rather strident disavowal of the trend towards more education may be found in some quarters. For example, 'Critics of this entire trend, the industrious and hard-working people of all walks of life, the elitists if you like, will continue to view the products of this prolonged education as giant babies, as dependent, incompetent slobs, or drug addicts, commies, and psychotics' (Toman 1972).

In western societies there has been a tendency to regard work and leisure as segregated activities. In the future they may become complementary and interdependent.

... The long range goal is not only to maximize leisure time but also to fuse it with a uniquely satisfying form of work ... In this fusion, work may lose its present characteristic feature of constraint and gain the creativity now associated mainly with leisure, while leisure may lose its present characteristic feature of opposition to work and gain the status – associated mainly with the *product* of work – of a resource worthy of planning to provide the greatest possible human satisfaction. (Hollander quoted in Parker 1972 p 122)

Such fine words notwithstanding, we wonder to what extent such changes are a potential reality. Stanley Parker comments that 'by the standards of those whose work has reasonable scope for personal involvement, there are relatively few jobs today which reach these standards' (Parker 1972 p 112), although he goes on to query to what extent the proportion of jobs which people regard as 'worthy' of personal involvement is immutable. On the one hand many jobs are becoming more routine and mechanical, but on the other hand many of these may be eventually automated. Furthermore, it is very possible that the shift towards tertiary service jobs will continue and as long as these are not mostly of the more menial type of service occupation, such a shift may presage once again an era of more rewarding work. We may even return to a more craft-orientated type of specialized work akin to that of pre-industrial society but at a much higher level now that we are reaping the rewards of the industrial era. The growth of small shops selling handmade pottery, leather work, clothing, etc. provides one indication.

What are the likely implications of a shift in the nature of, and the attitudes towards work? A major one is a diminution of the importance attached to location in relation to place of work. As work plays a declining role in human activity – at least in terms of time expended – we might reasonably expect a freeing of place of residence from the straitjacket imposed by the journey to work. Amenity rather than accessibility may come to play the leading role in the location of economic activities as we saw in Section 3. Although industry may not be 'footloose' today or in the immediate future, it is closely related to the distribution of population and changes in this distribution could and have engendered locational changes in industry.

The population-industrial location relationship is not simply one-way, however. It is more of a reciprocal arrangement, and thus a freeing of locational constraints for industry could result in a considerable redistribution of population. A decline in the interdependence of workplace and residence will be largely effected by technological changes especially in transport and communication. It is to these that we now turn.

SAQ 4 Suggest the possible directions of change resulting from increasing automation.

SAQ 5 What forces might counteract these trends?

5.3 Technological changes

It is self-evident but important that technological change embraces a multitude of areas and possibilities. This poses the problem of selection, and the specification of the criteria upon which selection should be based. To include those facets of technological change that are likely to impinge or affect the future urban society is to include virtually everything, for contemporary western societies are almost wholly urban societies. Here we shall focus on those aspects that will influence the future spatial organization and which can be modified or controlled through urban planning. The potential spatial outcomes will be the subject of Unit 31.

5.3.1 Changes in building technology

The future shape and density of cities will depend, in part, on building technology and economics (See Unit 15). Prior to the invention of the lift in 1859, the height of residential and commercial buildings was restricted. The lift enabled the development of the skyscraper, the first of which was built in Chicago in 1885. Although lifts demand space and energy, high rise buildings compensate for this by potentially more efficient use of heating and cooling systems. The imagined advantage of high rise building was the increase in densities. It was thought that these would enable a saving in the demand for agricultural land, more intensive use of high cost building land, and the retention of people (and hence votes and rates) within existing local authority boundaries.

High rise residential buildings did not reach Britain until the late 1950s and early 1960s, where, by and large, they have been associated with the comprehensive redevelopment of the decaying inner areas of cities. Following as they did in the wake of the extensive planning controls inaugurated by the Town and Country Planning Act of 1947, they were seen as the antidote to the suburban expansion of the 1920s and 1930s. High rise building was encouraged by the system of housing subsidies and new methods of construction including system building, ie prefabricated units for erection on site. Aesthetic attitudes played their part and estates such as Roehampton (Figure 3) were highly regarded by architects for their layout and design. By the late 1960s the

Figure 3 Roehampton Source: Greater London Council Photographic Library

economic case in favour of high rise buildings was being questioned. Both Stone (1961 and 1969b) and Best (1965) argued that the savings in land costs that accrued through higher densities were far outweighed by the extra costs of construction and maintenance. Stone's evidence demonstrated that two-storey blocks were cheapest, with a steep rise in costs up to five storeys, followed by a more modest rise in costs with each additional storey. His findings related not only to building costs, but to the costs of maintenance and servicing, and the cost of providing open space, roads and communal services. He concluded that the cost of high density is rarely worthwhile from an economic point of view unless the occupiers place a very high value on living in blocks of flats (for which there is very little evidence) or high density development reduces overspill sufficiently for travelling and other costs to offset the higher costs of development (Stone 1969a in Reader). But it was the sociological arguments that proved decisive in provoking a reaction against high rise flats in Britain. Various surveys undertaken during the 1960s highlighted the problem of children's play, of general lack of amenity, of conflict produced through incompatibility among neighbours, and of loneliness especially among old people. The Ronan Point disaster of 1968 when a gas explosion caused the collapse of part of a tower block in Canning Town in east London brought the debate about high rise living to the public notice. The decline in high rise building since that time is revealed in the statistics – in 1967 fourteen per cent of the dwellings constructed by local authorities and new town corporations were of ten or more storeys. In 1968 (the year of Ronan Point) the proportion was nine per cent after which it dropped to six per cent (1969) and three per cent (1970 and 1971).

Figure 4 Ronan Point, Canning Town, East London: After the explosion Source: Keystone Press Agency

The high rise debate is now largely over though advocates of high rise in the tradition of le Corbusier (Reader) may still be found. The emphasis of British housing policies has swung in favour of rehabilitating the older housing stock wherever possible and of low rise, high density redevelopment wherever clearance is necessary. The only high rise residential building still occurring is that for high rent central city prestige blocks on extremely high cost land such as the Barbican in London (see part cover, Unit 8).

Figure 5 Low rise, high density redevelopment in hand   Source: RIBA Photographic Library

Although it may be technologically feasible to build at high density it is not always economically practicable or socially desirable to do so. Two-mile high cities can be built. The question is, are there good grounds for having them in the future? In most cases the answer is clearly no, and if we allow either technology or visionary schemes to determine our future environment we are flying in the face of common sense.

SAQ 6   What were the arguments in favour of high rise buildings in Britain?

SAQ 7   What were the arguments against high rise buildings in Britain?

5.3.2 Changes in transportation technology

A major problem of growing affluence in western cities has been the growth in car ownership and the consequent congestion and pollution of city centres. The Buchanan Report's figures (quoted earlier) predict a saturation level of thirty million cars in Britain by the end of the century. The conventional approach to the problem of congestion has, until recently, involved the construction of more roads, especially large scale urban motorways such as those to be seen in Birmingham or Glasgow. Fleisher identifies the fundamental dilemma of such a strategy:

. . . Congestion does not behave like a simple symptom of malfunction; otherwise, its reduction would be largely a matter of adding capacity. A new road is the standard solution, but in fact it is not often valid because the subsequent traffic becomes even more intense . . . In this respect, the network of highways resembles a system with de-stabilizing feedbacks. (Fleisher 1961 p 58)

Apart from the deficiencies of this 'solution' to the problem it also has the side-effect of destroying a significant proportion of urban-fabric, whilst creating high levels of environmental dis-amenity. Whilst it is perhaps not a fair example in that Los Angeles is essentially a product of the auto-age and has never possessed anything akin to the traditional city centre, seventy per cent of 'downtown' Los Angeles is given over to the car by way of freeways interchanges, car parks and the like (see Figure 6). The problem is rather different in western Europe and the older cities of the north-eastern United States, for there city centres existed before the motor age, and conservation and the car have become increasingly incompatible.

Figure 6 Car parking facilities: Wilshire Boulevard, downtown Los Angeles Source: Edward Ruscha

The car is an inefficient vehicle where mass movement within a confined area is concerned. As Unit 17 points out, to transport 5,000 persons along a given route in a short time period would require some 3,000 cars at the average load 1.6 persons, 70 to 90 buses, or 5 or 6 trains. As a bus only occupies about as much road space as 2.5 average cars, it would require fourteen times as much road space to move the people by car rather than bus.

The alternative is a reserved bus lane or tram track which can carry five to ten times as many persons as could normally travel in private cars at three people to every two cars in an ordinary road lane during peak periods. A railway track can carry up to fifty times as many people as the road lane. Several twelve and eighteen lane motorways would be required to replace the underground arteries of London, assuming car ownership was adequate.

As Fleisher puts it 'The city at present may exhibit the first occasion in history of a society suffering from an excess of local mobility'. Outside city centres the car possesses considerable advantages. It is such 'a fairly small, independent, self-powered and highly manoeuvrable means of getting about at ground level for both people and goods, that it is unlikely we shall ever wish to abandon it' (Buchanan 1964 p 33). This is the nub of the problem. The private car is not an unmitigated evil, it does offer tremendous advantages with regard to personal mobility.

Given this analysis of the problem we are confronted with a choice. On the one hand we can do nothing and wait and see what happens. This is an essentially fatalistic solution and does not accord with the view we have adopted in this block, namely that we must not only anticipate the future but act to control it where possible.

The alternative requires a change of policy. If the assumption of an unrestrained increase in traffic is relaxed then a combination of legislative and physical controls to achieve an efficient circulation of people in city centres is possible. Such controls might include higher car parking charges, fewer parking spaces, new forms of vehicle taxation and restricted access. But they would need to be complemented by improvements in the public transport system (improved services, new designs, changes in the fare structure), and in the environment of city centres. Various schemes have been introduced in British cities and these suggest a new direction in urban transport planning.

The decision on a transportation strategy for any city is not a purely economic one: it is fundamentally political. A choice is likely to confer benefits on one section of the population while demanding sacrifices of another (a point made in Unit 29). Inner city road improvement schemes are a commonly quoted example for they tend to benefit car users (at least in the short term) at the expense of a local population where housing and social networks are destroyed. On a wider scale such improvements will be likely to encourage travel by private car rather than by public transport, and this may necessitate more road schemes, a declining public transport service, increasing environmental damage and so on. Ultimately, these decisions taken together may effect a redistribution of real income in the community as a whole (the main theme of Harvey's article in Stewart 1972).

In the long term there are three directions in which the pattern of urban transportation might be changed. One is through changes in the social structure:

... If all the movements of every individual were controlled throughout the day, week and month, current transportation facilities could more than handle the total demands for travel. (Hanson 1966)

But 'The social costs of such manipulations are prohibitive ... in a society in which individual desires theoretically dominate all other considerations'. Another possibility is a change in urban forms.

... The physical environment which we now use was built when transportation acted as a locational constraint to a much greater degree than it now does. Today we enjoy an unprecedented freedom in choice of location for all types of activities, but the old physical structure of the city sometimes hampers our mobility. Urban transportation could be improved by decreasing the spatial convergence of trips and increasing the proximity of opportunities to satisfy the reasons for trips. (Hanson 1966)

As Unit 31 explains, in the future the urban form is likely to exhibit considerably more dispersal than is presently the case. As Units 13 and 24 indicated, both population and industry are decentralizing, and as cities grow in size this tendency will be reinforced. Thus, many journeys to work would be orbital journeys rather than radial ones. Even the continuing concentration of executive and decision making functions in the CBD postulated in Unit 12 would be unlikely to pose severe problems, for we would envisage that such individuals would choose to reside either in the central or inner city close to their work (see Unit 8) or in more remote locations (see Unit 24) commuting in by high speed rail transport. Furthermore, very large highly centralized metropolises are unlikely to evolve for ecological reasons. Their support systems would have to be of such a degree of complexity that any failure in them could prove disastrous. Power, waste-disposal, or transportation failures could lead to near paralysis.

A third possibility lies in changing transportation technology. This 'has the least cost in terms of intrinsic social values, although its immediate costs may be high' (Hanson 1966). Rather than detail the possible innovations and their roles here, you are referred to Unit 17, Section 4, 'Types and forms of urban transportation'. Already in many cities various new systems are being experimented with or developed. They include unrestricted use of cars in the suburbs combined with 'dial a bus'; automatic guideways for cars journeying into the city centre allied with some buses; and bus only routes and personal mass transit systems in the central city. Along with the development of rapid

Figure 7 **New developments in urban transportation** Numerous experiments designed to increase the speed and flexibility of the conventional bus have been introduced in various British cities. For example, Stevenage operates a 'Superbus' limited stop, flat fare service (a). Among the innovations that may transform urban transportation is the Personal Rapid Transit System that combines the flexibility of personal transport with the high capacity flows of public transport (b). These small (4-10 persons) automatically controlled cars run on guideways with optional stops at frequent intervals. The whole system can be fitted unobtrusively into the existing built environment (c).
Source: Transportation Technology Inc.

a

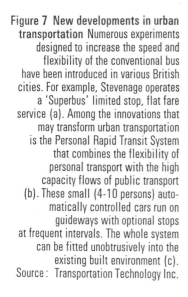

b   c

mass-transit systems in those cities now without them, these proposals may be said to represent likely possibilities. It should be borne in mind, however, that the gap between possibility and actuality remains a gap unless decisions are made and actions are taken. The technology exists. It is merely the will and the hard cash to back it that remain wanting.

SAQ 8   What are the relative advantages and disadvantages of public and private transport?

SAQ 9   How could the pattern of urban transportation be altered in the long run?

5.3.3 Changes in communications technology

Current developments in the field of telecommunications have been discussed in some detail in Unit 18. In the Reader you will find an article by J. S. Whyte (1970) which projects some of these developments into the future. In the final section of the Reader the article by Leicester imagines the effect such developments will have for the individual. This is taken a step further by Huxley and Forster who speculate on the social implications of technological change. Together these extracts provoke important questions as to the consequences of the course we choose.

In terms of specific developments Goldmark (1972a) has outlined four basic telecommunication networks which he sees as comprising the nervous system of a 'wired city'. The first, or primary network, already exists in embryo in the telephone. With the expansion of this system to include pictures we have the videophone. The PO is already well advanced in developing this commercially. It is, as Goldmark notes, a full, two-way random-access network, whose basic attribute is its ability to put anyone (or any machine) in touch with anyone else (or any other machine). It will enable the transmission of voice and data, and pictures and written materials.

The second network would be a broad band multi-channel cable television network with a limited response system. According to Goldmark, it would 'take over the task of distributing information in bulk from central facilities to offices and homes. It would, in effect, be an alternative way of receiving the information that now comes through books, records, broadcasting and so on'. Its chief advantage over conventional broadcasting systems is the degree of selectivity it permits. As Parker and Dunn describe it:

. . . Broadcast television is like the passenger railroad, taking people to scheduled places at scheduled times. Cable television has the potential of becoming like a highway network, permitting people to use their television sets in the way they use their personal automobiles; they may be able to select information, education, and entertainment at times and places of their own choosing. (Parker and Dunn 1972)

As of January 1971, there were 60 million households with television sets in the United States, 5.3 million of which were served by cable TV. If the rate of growth over the period 1966–71 is continued, then by 1980 the number of households served by cable TV *could* be 30 million.

The third network could be another multi-channel broad band connecting the major public institutions of the city into an integrated information network, and the fourth would be a sensing network to ensure greater feedback and hence control over such things as traffic conditions. In addition to internal communication networks which we have briefly described, the wired city of the future will also have certain *external* networks linking it to other cities or countries. These developments will intensify the changes in work patterns to which we have already referred. Information will become the critical requirement as economies shift in their emphasis from manufacturing to service occupations. Many people will be able to work in their homes, or in a local office, transacting their business either by videophone or by cable TV. If several individuals wish to discuss a problem together they will, perhaps, utilize 'confravision'. Currently being tested by the PO, this device links several people into one large videophone hook-up (Unit 18).

Much the same is true educationally, and in this area the Open University itself is a pioneer. Even with the OU, however, printed units like this one are distributed physically, tutors and students congregate physically at study centres, and programmes are broadcast on a fixed basis. In addition if you wish to consult a paper not supplied in the form of a Reader or Supplementary Material, you have to go to a library. In the 'wired city', however, programmes might be held in a central data library, to be called up whenever you wish. So too, all major books and papers in a field might be micro-filmed, so that they could be called up using a 'frame-grabber'. This device takes its name from its ability to take a single television picture (or frame) lasting 1/30th of a second, 'grab' it out of all the other frames being transmitted on a cable, and then repeatedly supply it to the set so that the viewer sees this frame as a still-picture on the set. Furthermore, students would be able to call other students and/or tutors and hold seminars using confravision – a hook-up videophone device which interconnects several people.

Parker and Dunn point out one major caveat here, however; the informational equivalent of the poverty gap. 'If access to these information services is not universally available throughout the society, then those already "information-rich" may reap the benefits while the "information-poor" get relatively poorer' (Parker and Dunn 1972).

Universal access to information, on the other hand, enable the economically, culturally, or politically deprived to gain useful and relevant information. In addition, the low-cost, large-capacity, and local nature of cable television relative to conventional broadcasting may enable a great deal more community participation in community decision making. Minority groups could have far greater access to the media than they now have though Parker and Dunn point out that legal guarantees of non-discriminative access would be needed. As well as these economic, educational, social and political advantages to be derived from the wired city, Parker and Dunn suggest that the trend towards the substitution of information for mobility could slow down the rate of energy consumption and pollution creation. How true this is is open to question. Certainly some suggest that the growth of the telephone leads to more mobility rather than less, in that it enables people to make arrangements to meet or travel more easily.

5.3.4 The spatial implications of technological change

The ultimate development of the total replacement of mobility by electrical communications is the isolation and immobility depicted in E. M. Forster's *The Machine Stops* (see Reader) where all first-hand experience is terminated. Forster's narrative is a warning rather than a prediction. It is possible that greater personal mobility and the development of telecommunications could lead to the reversal of the present pattern of settlement. Instead of densely populated urban regions surrounded by declining, sparsely populated peripheries, there may be declining urban regions and expanding peripheries. In any case the further territorial expansion of settlements is likely as the friction of distance is reduced. Such a trend is welcomed by advocates of a 'New Rural Society' in which small villages and towns replace the major conurbations of today. Goldmark believes this would rid American cities of racial conflict (Goldmark 1972b). *A Blueprint for Survival* (see Reader extract) echoes this viewpoint believing decentralization to be the essential prelude to a stable society. Both ignore the fact that it is not size *per se* that is the underlying cause of social problems, but rather the nature of society itself.

We would question the view that decentralization will be the outcome of technological change. After all the postal service and the telephone appear to have increased the need for face-to-face communication. The telephone may have contributed to the suburban exodus but it was only feasible when a new means of personal transportation had been discovered. Fleisher doubts that the videophone or cable TV are likely to have as much influence as the telephone, arguing 'The difference the telephone created is very much larger than the added advantage of a television channel' (Fleisher 1961 p 54). Personally, we do not think that any definitive answer can be given to the likely influence of telecommunications on the pattern of density and settlements. If pressed, we would probably agree with both Webber and Fleisher that new technological developments are, in themselves, spatially neutral. As Webber says 'They could push urban spatial structure towards greater concentricity, toward greater dispersion, or, what I believe to be most likely, toward a very heterogeneous pattern' (Webber 1963).You should read Whyte and Goldmark in the Reader and Webber's article in Bourne (1971) and try to make up your own minds.

5.3.5 The psychological implications of technological change

Psychological factors may also prove an important source of resistance to decentralization in the future. The concentration of population is conventionally explained as a function of the accessibility needed for the efficient and economic exchange of goods and services. We believe that the socio-psychological aspects of concentration or dispersal have been neglected.

To live at very low density, or even in isolation, is not the same as living in a traditional town or city, even with the possibility of instantaneous worldwide electronic communication. Contacts have to be directed, planned and perhaps pre-arranged. There would be fewer random encounters with people,

Figure 8 Life in the city centre   Source: Keystone Press Agency

Figures 9a and 9b Quiescent suburbia Source: (b) Keystone Press Agency

a   b

ideas or things which is a characteristic of city life. Bellan comments of the
large city that its 'variety stimulates; numerous heterogeneous and changing
elements combine in a constant succession of new and interesting amalgams
that liven the local outlook and widen its horizons' (Bellan 1966 p 177). The
city generally offers what the centralists (see Unit 8) seek writ large in the central
and inner city – its easily perceived sense of activity; its vitality and pulse of
life.

It is a matter for conjecture whether these attributes would be present in the
dispersed or very low density settlements. Webber (1963) and Hall (1968b)
would both maintain that a six mile 10 minute journey by car on the urban
freeway is no more than a 10 minute walk round the block. Webber comments,
'spatial separation or propinquity is no longer an adequate indicator of
functional relations'. This we would not dispute. We would, however, dispute
that:

. . . When people can interact with others across great distances and when they can
readily move themselves into face-to-face positions as the need to do so arises, it
hardly matters whether the space between them and their associates is used for houses
and factories. (Webber 1963 p 49)

Webber and Bellan represent opposite ends of the spectrum. Some people are
highly gregarious and choose (if they can) to live in the city. Others may prefer
the space that living in the country affords. Whatever the individual preferences
it is unlikely that telecommunications could ever wholly substitute for face-to-
face contact. There is surely a qualitative as well as a quantitative difference
between the two. Apart from the fact that certain behavioural nuances are
unlikely to ever be picked up electronically, we would suggest that the very
knowledge that an individual is dealing with an image rather than a person in
the flesh, is likely to result in certain changes in behaviour. Communication

may, for example, be more aggressive or less intimate. 'It may not be adequate for transactions that would terminate in a handshake or a fist fight. Clearly it would not suffice for encounters that culminate in an embrace' (Fleisher 1961 p 53).

SAQ 10   What changes of urban form may result from the development of communications?

SAQ 11   What factors will constrain these changes?

6 Changes in the social structure

Like technological change, social change has many facets. It is only possible to consider certain broad changes here, those which we think particularly relevant to the organization and pattern of future urban society. Obviously, it is impossible to isolate specifically social changes from their economic or environmental context. Similarly some of the changes we have already considered under other heads, such as leisure or communications have strong social connotations. Here we shall look at the potential change in the social structure, spatial organization, and life styles of the future city.

6.1 Changes in family structure

In the family structure there has been considerable change. Over the past fifty years the importance of the 'extended family' (ie three or more generations) in the social structure has diminished. It survives, notably in the 'urban village' (Unit 7) where consanguinity and propinquity are combined. The nuclear family, living in separate accommodation, and often at some distance from relatives, has become the basic social unit of urban society, and the rate of new household formation has increased recently. Life styles and the housing and consumer goods that support them have focused around the small family. Increased rates of marriage, earlier marriage, fewer children, and longer survival have increased the interdependence of conjugal partners. Their roles are less segregated and more equal. At the same time marital breakdowns have increased, and some have predicted a shift away from the nuclear family towards a more varied form of social organization such as communal ones. Willmott, however, takes the view that 'what seems more likely is that, with some modification, the shift to home-centredness and family-centredness will continue' (Willmott 1969 p 296). Indeed, some consider that our very survival depends upon it, 'the family which clearly represents the first level of human organization, is a universal feature of all human societies, and there is no example of its suppression without the most serious social consequences' (Ecologist 1972). By contrast the nuclear family is sometimes regarded as the chief obstacle to social progress, a barrier to the communal, egalitarian principles of the ideal society. Whatever the valuations placed upon the family as a social unit, we may be sure that if major changes do occur in this area, they will have a profound effect upon the nature of the future society, and hence upon the future city.

6.2 Changes in the distribution of wealth and income

The pattern of income distribution in any society is a major determinant of its pattern of consumption and hence of its social and spatial structure. Willmott (in Reader) notes a number of persistent economic and social features in British society. Among these are features that support the system of social stratification. For example, the proportion of manual workers in the population changed little during the first half of the twentieth century. The proportion of working class children in the total population entering university rose at about the same rate as that for middle class children. Overall, the distribution of wealth shifted little with five per cent of the population still owning at least a half of the total personal wealth in 1960. He concludes that 'despite some changes, the social structure has, in some of the essentials remained extraordinarily constant' (Willmott 1969 p 288). But, looked at another way these statistics also betray considerable change, though at an absolute rather than at a relative level. The manual working force does different kinds of work, is more skilled, and contains a larger number of women than was the case at the beginning of the century. The proportion of children attending university rose two and a half times between 1928 and 1960. Real incomes have risen during the period. There is, therefore, the apparent paradox of stability within a changing situation which Willmott does not consider will alter much in the immediate future, 'though all will be richer, "inequality" will not be reduced, indeed it may well increase' (Willmott 1969). (See Figure 10 and Table 1.)

Figure 10 The distribution of income, 1966   Source of data: Board of Inland Revenue

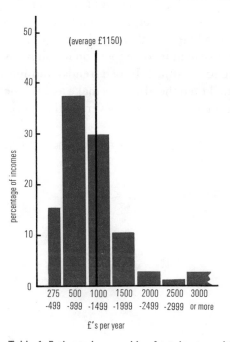

£'s per year

Table 1 Estimated ownership of total net wealth in Great Britain 1960–8, by various percentile groupings

Percentile group	1960	1961	1962	1963	1964	1965	1966	1967	1968
Largest 1%	27	28	26	26	25	24	22	23	24
Largest 5%	51	50	49	50	48	46	43	43	46
Smallest 80%	26	26	27	25	27	28	29	31	29
Smallest 50%	4	4	5	5	8	9	11	11	10
Gini coefficient of concentration %	76	72	72	73	72	70	67	67	68

Source: *Labour and Inequality*, Michael Meacher p 187

N.B. It is conventional wisdom that the richest 1 per cent of the population owns about a quarter of the wealth of Britain, that 5 per cent owns roughly half and that 20 per cent own virtually three-quarters. Estimates made by *The Economist* (15 January 1966) using the technique of capitalizing investment income, however, indicated that the richest 1 per cent owned 40 per cent of the total wealth, 2 per cent owned 55 per cent, and 7 per cent owned 84 per cent. Indeed, the richest *tenth of one per cent* was actually found to own 13 per cent of total wealth, a sum of £7,033 million, representing an average fortune of rather over one-third of a million pounds each.

Such inequality carries many implications of which we refer to just two, both of which will affect the future urban form, the subject of Unit 31. First there is the question of mobility. Despite the rapid rise in car ownership a considerable minority of the future urban society will not have access to a car.

Even when car ownership reaches the 'saturation' level[1] the old, infirm, children and housewives (where the husband uses the car for work) will be deprived of access to a car for much of the time. A ratio of 1.3 cars per family implies that many families in 2010 will not possess a car or will (if current trends continue) become increasingly disadvantaged as alternative means of transport disappear. Similarly, travel and foreign tourism are unlikely to diffuse totally down through the various income strata. For all the much vaunted mobility of Americans, only about thirty per cent have ever made a plane journey (Davidoff in Reader).

Second, there is the question of housing. In some capitalist economies home ownership is a major social goal. In Britain only just over half the households have achieved this. There has not been a close correspondence between the rise in house prices and incomes. During the late 1960s incomes tended to rise faster but the situation was reversed in the early 1970s culminating in the great inflation of house prices in 1972 (see Figure 11). Lovell and Nightingale (1972) suggest that such a trend is unlikely to persist 'unless the proportion of income which owner occupiers spend on housing were to increase much more rapidly than it has in the past'. There is some fragmentary evidence that the proportion of household income spent on housing has increased and in parts of London is up to one-third. If such trends continue and the rise in house prices is sustained then the ability to make a first time purchase of housing for owner occupation will shrink to the very highest income groups, or those with private means.

Figure 11 New house prices Source: Research Memorandum 384, Department of Planning and Transportation GLC 1972 Figure 6

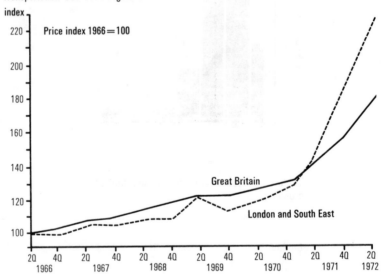

For the most affluent groups, second home ownership will become more common in the future enabling them to combine urban living with weekend and holiday recreation in the country. But for the urban poor the prospect of home ownership, let alone a second home, is remote. Indeed, in the major cities the prospect of satisfactory housing is diminishing for many people. It is here that housing shortage is most acute and housing standards are most depressed. There is the very real possibility that, despite rising incomes and aspirations, the quality and space standards of housing in parts of the major cities will continue to deteriorate.

[1] ie 'when the ratio of cars to population ceases to show a material annual increase. For Britain as a whole it appears that this situation . . . may be reached in about 2010 when the ratio may stand at about 400 cars per 1,000 population.' (Buchanan Report)

All this presupposes that existing inequalities in wealth will persist, and perhaps even increase. Certainly, on past evidence, there has been little fundamental redistribution although all sections of society have shared in the absolute increase in wealth. We have, therefore, presented here an essentially conservative projection of the future. Any other prospect will require a change in social attitudes towards more equality, and the political will to enforce it.

6.3 Changing patterns of social segregation

Inequalities within a city find their spatial expression in the segregation that occurs, and access to the housing market endows the affluent with a choice of residence. The lower one moves down the social scale the more progressively restricted becomes the choice of where to live. In America the wealthy tend to shun the city and seek the suburbs 'where people with enough cash for the down payment on a house can shelter from the changes that have spoiled life elsewhere' (Davie 1972 in Reader). This trend has been largely responsible for the problem of the American city – its declining employment, falling tax base and decaying environment. The inner city is the habitat of the poor, or those who are deprived by virtue of their race. They are areas of violence which in the future may be literally sealed off from the rest of the city. Gold (1970) foresees the sealing off of CBDs during the hours of darkness, rooftop closed circuit TV enabling surveillance; the development of expressways as high speed 'sanitized corridors' connecting one safe area with another; and the actual fortification of buildings (see Figure 12). He states, though, that:

. . . The physical distance of suburban neighbourhoods from central cities is the principal way that suburban residents are protected against crime. Distance substitutes for and is more effective than other deterrent features in central cities. (Gold 1970)

Overall, Gold views such developments as wholly detrimental. He believes that such defensive use of the urban environment will not attack the cause or roots of crime but compound them by preventing any communication or mutual understanding developing between groups. In addition it will reduce everyone's freedom of choice, activity and movement in the city.

Figure 12 Defensive architecture in the city centre   Source: Associated Press

In Britain the problem is rather different. In some parts of the inner city (Unit 8) there has been an influx of 'gentrifiers' (ie middle class people) into certain traditionally working class but architecturally desirable areas. The prospect of a poor inner city ghetto along American lines (Unit 9) is diminishing, if indeed it was ever a reality here. Indeed, there is the possibility of a partial reversal of the traditional pattern (if the trend continues) with the working classes being displaced from the inner city towards the periphery along pre-industrial lines. The development of large council estates in the outer suburbs of major cities provides some social variation even if social segregation in these areas remains marked (see Units 7 and 29).

Suburban areas, whatever their social differences tended in the past to be broadly similar in age composition. In the future this is less likely to be so. Each generation is growing up with quite distinct norms and values with respect to culture, work, leisure, social behaviour and so forth. Whatever the specific causes of these differences, they appear to be reflected to an increasing degree in segregation by age. 'There are suburbs occupied largely by young married couples with small children, or by middle-aged couples with teenagers, or by older couples whose children have already left home. We have specially designed "retirement communities" for retirees' (quoted in *Sunday Times*, 3 Jan 1971).

What are the root reasons behind this development? Toman suggests that the pressures of modern life are becoming more intense and people seek refuge in order to retain their sense of identity. Clearly, with the older residents a large element of retreatism is involved. They are hoping, in a sense, that the problems of the real world will disappear. The phrase 'out of sight out of mind' aptly sums this up. Also many people are moving to developments where, as one put it, 'You'll know the sort of people who'll be your neighbour'. It appears that increasing intolerance of differences plays a part. One American developer remarked that 'Put young marrieds with infants in the same development with single people and old couples, and you wind up with an almost impossible mixture. What we're interested in is renting to people who have compatible, not conflicting interests'. Another developer, however, admitted that 'specialized housing may ultimately be a dangerous development . . . It may well contribute to the general breakdown in communication between different levels of society. But there's no getting round the fact that "life style" housing is the thing of the future because rightly or wrongly, that's what Americans want. It's inevitable' (quoted in *Sunday Times*, 3 Jan 1971).

We commented earlier in the unit on the dangers of confusing inexorable trends with inevitable trends. In the future 'it could eventually be possible to pass from early adulthood to old age without ever having to suffer neighbours of a different generation, background, or colour' (*Sunday Times*, 3 Jan 1971). If that happens the potential social divisiveness becomes almost unlimited. But such a trend is not inevitable though we must act to arrest it by encouraging greater social integration. As Unit 29 has shown up to a certain point, propinquity can promote understanding while segregation encourages suspicion and hostility. But the argument can be pursued too far for complete integration can bring about the isolation of individuals or conflict among them.

Even in socialist societies where income disparities are less marked, a latent process of segregation according to age and occupation can be discerned (TV programmes 14 and 15 and Musil in Pahl 1968). Here differences in status are derived from education and occupation and they are manifested in differences in life styles.

The most important change in life styles is that there are likely to be more of them. The rising standard of living in contemporary western urban-industrial society has increased the individual's range of choice of where and how he lives. The greater *per capita* wealth, leisure and energy within these societies can thus be expended in any of a variety of ways. Bell postulated three: familism, careerism and consumerism, and found a fourth, the search for community (Bell 1968). The even greater increases in income and leisure time over the next thirty years are likely to increase the number of choices far more than ever before. McElrath, for example, foresees a growing diversification, as does Webber who says 'Rather than a "mass culture" in a "mass society" the long term prospect is for a maze of subcultures within an amazingly diverse society organized upon a broadly shared cultural base'. We are certainly witnessing a rapid increase in interest and activity based groups along with specific locational groups. Among these are the conservation societies, the motorway and community action groups who have begun to make such an impression on the physical development of cities.

It is not the peculiarities of life styles that interest us *per se*. Life styles are frequently manifested in location. Different areas possess different utilities for different groups depending on their differing needs and wants. The opportunities for divergent life styles, and therefore the choices that can be made, are growing in western societies. Even here there are large groups of the underprivileged for whom little choice exists. Elsewhere, in the developing countries, economic constraints impose a traditional way of life on the majority of the population. In the communist world conformity is imposed as a necessary condition of economic development.

If and when the disparities that exist within all societies are narrowed or overcome, greater attention may be paid to the quality of the urban environment. For the affluent this is already an important issue and explains the flourishing of amenity groups to represent their values. For the poor the problems of subsistence are paramount. According to Mishan 'once physical subsistence is assumed . . . the most important single element in man's welfare is the environment in which he lives' (Mishan 1972 p 109). As incomes rise so people are likely to become increasingly dissatisfied with their urban environment. Making cities capable of satisfying not just human needs but our aspirations as well is one of the most important challenges of the future.

SAQ 12   What impact is a changing family structure likely to have on the city of the future?

SAQ 13   What spatial disadvantages are the poorer sections of society likely to experience in the city of the future?

SAQ 14   What processes are responsible for the trend towards segregation in cities?

SAQ 15   How far can these processes be modified?

7 Conclusion

In this unit we have examined a variety of changes, both probable and possible, likely to differentiate the future urban society from the societies of today, subject to various constraints. We may be certain, however, that some of these changes may not occur, just as others not considered here may equally well do so. So too certain constraints may disappear, and fresh ones pose themselves. Some of the changes we envisage may not seem overly exciting, but we must beware of posing what Emrys Jones terms 'maximal changes' merely for their intrinsic excitement. It is far more important to outline realistic probabilities than remote but exotic possibilities. To do so would be to depart from the tradition of rigorous enquiry for the realms of fiction. As Jones states 'The future envisaged is a familiar one in so far as the present is seen as a point along a continuum from a known past to a probable future' (Jones 1969 p 342).

Just as there are some changes we have not, and perhaps could not, have considered, so too we have not examined in any detail the potential interactions and interrelationships between the changes we have conjectured. This is something you yourselves should attempt to do. We would warn, however, against an excess of faith in one or two simplifying abstractions or theories. Society is a complicated system and complexity rather than simplicity is likely to typify the future.

Finally, the future condition of society is not the inevitable outcome of present trends. We have tried to emphasize in this unit that there are alternative futures and that we must, inevitably, choose among them. There are some events which we as individuals can influence, others require a shift in social values. The path of least effort will be to co-operate with some of the inexorable trends we have outlined here. The most difficult but the more rewarding course will be to establish the desirable goals of urban development, and to formulate a means of achieving them. This is the problem that is taken up in the units which follow.

Answers to SAQs

Answer SAQ 1   A primary forecast is an attempt to predict a likely course of events in the absence of correcting action. A secondary forecast indicates the possible outcomes of specified correcting actions on the original phenomenon.

Answer SAQ 2   a Signalling – the future sequence of events will conform to an earlier one.
b Extrapolation – the extension of an existing tendency.
c Causality – the specification of the necessary effect of a causal factor.
d Analogy – the prediction is based on the similarity of one case to another.

Answer SAQ 3   Birth rates and death rates are the aggregates of individual births and deaths. But whereas the death rate is very stable, individual decisions as to the number of children and size of family can have, and have had, marked effects on the birth rate. This affects both the growth of the population and its structure in the sense that the dependency ratio (the ratio of the inactive to the active population) changes. Low birth rates lead to a relatively 'older' population, high birth rates to a relatively 'younger' one.

Answer SAQ 4   Increasing automation is likely to result in a shift from manual to non-manual occupations, in greater structural unemployment in the short term, and in an increase in leisure and associated opportunities in the longer term, such as non-vocational education. Finally, the importance of location relative to place of work could diminish in favour of location relative to amenities.

Answer SAQ 5   The trend towards greater leisure might be counteracted by an increase in overtime and the trend towards non-manual occupations by a return to more craft orientated types of work.

Answer SAQ 6   High rise buildings were thought to allow higher densities, a more intensive use of high cost building land, the retention of people, votes and rates within existing local authority boundaries and the preservation of agricultural land.

Answer SAQ 7   It was shown that the potential benefits to be gained in land costs and food production were smaller than had been assumed and relatively unimportant when set against the costs of construction and maintenance of high rise developments. The sociological problems of high rise living, highlighted at the time of the Ronan Point collapse, made the case against high rise buildings even more conclusive. Finally, high rise development came to be recognized as a poor solution to the problem of density, and low rise buildings were shown to enable equal, if not higher densities, to be achieved if correctly laid out.

Answer SAQ 8   Private transport as it currently exists permits – in theory – a high level of personal mobility allied with individual route selection and availability, and at all hours door-to-door travel. Problems arise when large numbers of private vehicles are concentrated together in existing cities. Not only are they inefficient as carriers and route-users, but they generate a high level of externalities in the form of congestion, noise, and atmospheric pollution. Public transport, on the other hand, is far more efficient both in terms of carrying capacity and route-utilization. Its deficiencies lie in its aggregate qualities – it lacks the instantaneous all hours availability and point to point route selection that personal transport permits. Furthermore, the quality of the service provided is largely dependent on the rate of usage. The higher the use, the better the service that can be provided.

Answer SAQ 9   Three alternative possibilities suggest themselves. First, whether or not to attempt to alter or control the behaviour of individuals and the social and economic organization of the city; secondly whether to alter the existing urban form; and thirdly, whether to change the actual transport technology employed. Of these possibilities the first is clearly ruled out in a free society. The second might prove impossible in the short run and costly in the longer term, while the third, though also expensive, offers more immediate prospects of success.

Answer SAQ 10   In the past, new modes of communication have tended to result in more concentrated settlements. Current and future improvements in communications technology should lead to a more decentralized and diffuse settlement structure, as the 'friction of space' is diminished. Some commentators even believe that a total reversal of the present pattern of settlement is likely, the declining inter-urban peripheries becoming the new growth areas.

Answer SAQ 11   The spatial diffusion of cities is likely to be constrained by various factors. First, there are the social and psychological forces associated with dense urban concentrations. Secondly, there is the constraint of the existing built environment. Thirdly, it is difficult to predict how far new developments in telecommunications will influence future urban form. The telephone and the postal systems have generated, if anything, even greater propinquity. The same could be true of current developments. Finally, as Fleisher points out, there are some things for which telecommunications can never substitute.

Answer SAQ 12   If by changing family structure we understand a continuing move away from extended family structures towards more nucleated ones, then the most immediate results will be an increase in the number of dwelling units required.

Small family units will become separated from their relatives and this may cause increasing mobility if visits are to be achieved. Some would predict a greater tendency to marital breakdown as families become more isolated. This could result in a move towards more communal types of organization and a consequent development of large dwellings. Willmott, however, considers the more likely trend to be towards further emphasis on the small family unit.

Answer SAQ 13 Poorer people are likely to remain segregated living in the decaying inner city areas. Relatively immobile, they are likely to suffer as jobs are decentralized to the affluent suburban areas, or as new access roads are forged through their residential areas to provide greater accessibility for the mobile sections of the community. Finally, crime and violence tend to be concentrated in the poorer, less protected parts of the city.

Answer SAQ 14 The root causes of the problem would appear to be inequality of income and opportunity, and the social stratification brought about both by higher incomes and mobility. People with choice tend to migrate to areas where the social composition conforms to their own, and in which they are free from the problems that exist elsewhere in the city. Fear, prejudice and intolerance play a large part in this mechanism, increasing differentiation leading to a desire for even more differentiation and segregation.

Answer SAQ 15 The modification of such processes would require fundamental changes in economic opportunities and social values. If anything it would take many years to halt and reverse them. Reductions in the level of inequalities in income, jobs and residences would play a major part, but changes in attitudes would be slower, and would in part depend upon the unity and cohesion of the society in question. Attempts to integrate different groups without parallel shifts in social attitudes are unlikely to overcome basic divisions as Unit 29 has shown.

References

ANDERSON, S. (ed) (1968) *Planning for diversity and choice*, Cambridge, Mass. MIT Press.

BELL, W. (1968) 'The City, the suburb, and a theory of social choice' in GREER, S. *et al* (eds) (1968) *The New Urbanization*, New York, St Martins Press, pp 132–68.

BELLAN, R. C. (1966) 'The Future Growth of Britain's Cities' in *Town Planning Review*, 37, pp 173–88.

BERRY, B. J. L. (1970) 'The Geography of the United States in the Year 2000' in *Transactions, Institute of British Geographers*, 51, pp 21–54.

BEST, R. (1964) 'The Future Urban Acreage' in *Town and Country Planning*, pp 350–5.

BEST, R. (1965) 'Recent changes and future prospects in land use in England and Wales' in *Geographical Journal*, 131.

BOURNE, L. S. (ed) (1971) *The Internal Structure of the City*, New York, Oxford University Press (set book).

BUCHANAN REPORT (1963) *Traffic in Towns*, London, HMSO; (1964) Penguin Books.

DAVIDOFF, P. (1968) 'Normative Planning' in ANDERSON, S. (ed) (1968) pp 173–9.

DAVIE, M. (1972) *In the Future Now*, London, Hamish Hamilton.

DE JOUVENEL, B. (1967) *The Art of Conjecture*, London, Weidenfeld and Nicholson.

ECOLOGIST (1972) *A Blueprint for Survival*, Harmondsworth, Penguin (originally published in *The Ecologist*, 2, 1, 1972).

FLEISHER, A. (1961) 'The Influence of Technology in Urban Forms' in *Daedalus*, Winter, 'The Future Metropolis'.

GOLD, R. (1970) 'Urban violence and contemporary defensive cities' in *Journal of the American Institute of Planners*, 36, 3, pp 146–59.

GOLDMARK, P. (1972a) 'Communications and the Community' in *Scientific American*, 227, 3, Sept, pp 142–50.

GOLDMARK, P. (1972b) 'Communications for a new rural society' in *Journal of the SMPTE*, 81, pp 512–17.

GOLDSMITH, E. (ed) (1971) *Can Britain Survive?* London, Stacey.

HALL, P. (1966) *The World Cities*, London, World University Library, Weidenfeld and Nicholson.

HALL, P. (1968a) 'Land use: the spread of towns into the country' in YOUNG, M. (ed) (1968).

HALL, P. (1968b) 'The Urban Culture and the Suburban Culture' in EELLS, R. and WALTON, C. (eds) (1969) *Man in the City of the Future*, London, Collier-Macmillan, pp 99–146.

HANSON, M. (ed) (1966) *Project Metran*, Cambridge, Mass. MIT Press.

JENCKS, C. (1971) *Architecture 2000*, London, Studio Vista.

JONES, E. (1969) 'Resources and Environmental Constraints' in *Urban Studies* 6, 3 (Special Issue: Developing Patterns of Urbanization).

KAHN, H. and WIENER, A. J. (1967) *The Year 2000*, London, Collier-Macmillan.

LE CORBUSIER (1924) 'The Contemporary City' in *The City of Tomorrow*, London, Architectural Press.

LOVELL, A. and NIGHTINGALE, J. R. (1972) 'Private Sector House Prices', Dept of Planning and Transportation, Research Memorandum 384, Greater London Council.

MEIER, R. (1969) 'Material Resources' in JUNGK, R. and GALTUNG, J. (1969) *Mankind 2000*, London, Allen and Unwin, pp 100–16.

MISHAN, E. J. (1972) 'Thinking of the Future' in HÄGERSTRAND, T. and VAN HULTEN, M. (eds) (1972) *Europe 2000: Fears and Hopes for European Urbanization*, The Hague, Martinus Nijhoff.

PARKER, E. B. and DUNN, D. A. (1972) 'Information Technology: Its Social Potential' in *Science*, 176, pp 1392–9.

PARKER, S. (1972) *The Future of Work and Leisure*, Paladin.

SNOW, C. P. (1959) *The Two Cultures and the Scientific Revolution*, London, Cambridge University Press.

STEWART, M. (ed) (1972) *The City: Problems of Planning*, Harmondsworth, Penguin Books (set book).

STONE, P. (1961) 'The Impact of Urban Development on the Use of Land and Other Resources' in *Journal of the Town Planning Institute*.

STONE, P. (1969a) 'Resources and the Economic Framework' in *Urban Studies*, 6, 3 (Special Issue: Developing Patterns of Urbanization).

STONE, P. (1969b) *Urban Development in Britain: Standards, Costs and Resources 1964–2004. Part 1 Population and Housing*, London, Cambridge University Press.

SUNDAY TIMES (1971) *The Affluent Ghetto*, 3 Jan 1971.

TILLINGHAST, P. (1968) 'Leisure: Old Patterns and New Problems' in ANDERSON, S. (ed) (1968) pp 143–53.

TOFFLER, A. (1970) *Future Shock*, London, The Bodley Head; also (1973) Pan Books (paperback).

TOMAN, W. (1972) 'Socio-Psychological Aspects' in HÄGERSTRAND, T. and VAN HULTEN, M. (eds) (1972) *Europe 2000: Fears and Hopes for European Urbanization*, The Hague, Martinus Nijhoff.

WEBBER, M. (1963) 'Order in Diversity: Community without Propinquity' in WINGO, L. (ed) *Cities and Space*, Baltimore, Johns Hopkins Press; (Paperback 1966).

WELLS, H. G. (1902) *Anticipations of the reactions of mechanical and scientific progress upon human life and thought*, London, Chapman and Hall.

WHITE, ORTRUDE (1969) 'Societal determinants of urban form – some thoughts on the city in the year 2000' in *Centre for Environmental Studies*, Working Paper 45.

WHYTE, B. S. (1970) *The Impact of Telecommunications on Town Planning*, Town and Country Planning Summer School, Swansea.

WILLMOTT, P. (1969) 'Some Social Trends' in *Urban Studies*, 6, 3 (Special Issue: Developing Patterns of Urbanization).

YOUNG, M. (ed) (1968) *Forecasting and the Social Sciences*, London, Heinemann.

Acknowledgements   Grateful acknowledgement is made to the following sources for material used in this unit:

Figure 1: D. Meadows for D. H. Meadows *et al*, *Limits to Growth*, Earth Island Publishers, London 1972; *Figure 2:* Reprinted by permission of Faber and Faber Ltd, from *Greater London* (eds J. T. Coppock and H. C. Prince); *Figure 3:* Greater London Council Photograph Library; *Figures 4, 8 and 9:* Keystone Press Agency; *Figure 5:* RIBA Photograph Library; *Figure 6:* Edward Ruscha; *Figure 7:* Transportation Technology Inc; *Figure 11:* Greater London Council for A. Lovell and J. R. Nightingale, 'Private Sector House Prices' in *Planning and Transportation Department Research Memorandum RM384*; *Figure 12:* Associated Press.
Table 1: Fabian Society for M. Meacher, 'Wealth: Labour's Achilles Heel' in *Labour and Inequality*.

Unit 31 The future urban form
Chris Hamnett

Part cover: Aerial view of an intersection of the Santa Monica and San Diego Freeways
Source: State of California Division of Highways (Department of Transportation)

The future urban form

Aims This unit has two overall aims:

1 The examination and assessment of a variety of possible urban forms in terms of certain specified criteria.

2 The description and analysis of the evolving urban form as depicted through both facts and figures and the conceptualizations of various writers.

These two general aims are roughly paralleled by Sections 1–5 inclusive and 6–9 inclusive. Within these broad aims there are several more detailed aims:

a A demonstration of why urban form *per se* is important, at each of three different scales.

b The provision and examination of a set of criteria upon which various forms may be evaluated.

c The provision of some idea of the variety of possible forms.

d The evaluation of some of these possibilities in terms of the criteria previously discussed.

e An examination of the new 'formal' possibilities opened up by the work of March and Martin.

f The provision of sufficient facts and figures to show the changes being experienced both by individual cities, the urban population and the urban settlement pattern as a whole.

g The description and analysis of various conceptualizations of urban growth and change that have been put forward.

Objectives You should on having read this unit and the required reading be able to:

1 Outline why form is considered important at the micro, meso and macro scale of urban development.

2 Recall at least five criteria for the evaluation of urban form at various scales, critically examine those advanced, and advance some of your own with justifications.

3 Set out a rough classification of possible urban forms at the meso scale.

4 Make your own evaluation of some of these forms in terms of both some of the criteria advanced and of your own criteria.

5 Specify the possibilities March and Martin's work would seem to allow, and assess these.

6 Recall the major characteristics of the evolving urban form such as scale, size, extent, form.

7 Recall each of the eight conceptualizations of the evolving urban form, described in the unit, and make some evaluation of their relative merits.

8 Have a clearer idea of:

a the possibilities open to urban society where its cities are concerned;

b current trends;

c the type(s) of development you would consider desirable both from a personal and a more general social point of view.

Reading guide 1 Lynch, Kevin (1961) 'The Future Metropolis' in *Daedalus*, Winter 1961. Lynch takes five 'ideal' urban forms and examines each of them in terms of a set of criteria suggested by him as being important. Although somewhat abstract, this paper is valuable for its scope, its detailed analysis and its future orientations.

2 Freidmann, John and Miller, John (1965) 'The Urban Field' in *Journal of the Institute of American Planners*, November 1965. Freidmann and Miller examine various conceptualizations of the evolving

urban field, only to reject them and put forward their own concept. Involving, as it does, a wider integration of town and country within an area of about 100 miles radius from major cities, this concept is a useful and realistic pointer to the future.

3 March, Lionel (1967) 'Homes Beyond the Fringe' in *RIBA Journal*, August 1967.
Both this paper and the next one illustrate the application of theoretical principles to concrete problems. Drawing on a variety of theoretical insights, March demonstrates the inherent wastefulness of current forms of urban development, advocating instead high density linear development both in the city and the country.

4 Martin, Sir Leslie (1972) 'The Grid as Generator' in March, L. and Martin, L. (eds) (1972) *Urban Space and Structure*, Cambridge University Press.
Martin's paper demonstrates the close interrelationship between different street grids, plot sizes and building heights. It shows how the balance has been lost in New York and many other cities, and indicates how the enlargement of the grid pattern and the plots can rationalize developments. Both this and the preceding paper are valuable in demonstrating how high densities are compatible with low-rise development.

5 Lynch, Kevin (1968) 'The Possible City' in Bourne, L. S. (ed) (1971) *Internal Structure of the City*, Oxford University Press (set book).
In this broad but short essay Lynch looks at the problems we face in the city, and suggests a variety of strategies we might adopt. These range from new ways of structuring cities, through methods of easing change to the utilization of new technologies. Finally, Lynch specifies the type of urban environment we should be moving towards: open environments where choice is maximized.

1 Introduction: Form – its importance and implications

It is necessary as a first step to ask what we mean by the term 'urban form', and to consider why it is important. It is my intention to use the term form very generally so as to encompass a variety of scales. These scales range from the urban settlement pattern as a whole – both regional, national and international – at the macro level, through the changing internal structure of the city at the meso level, to specific built forms and their interrelationships at the micro level. This classification of form – macro, meso and micro – corresponds reasonably well with the distinctions 'on the ground'. It is not exclusive, however, and variations and suggested innovations at one scale frequently have implications for urban form at other scales.

Form is important at all three scales for a variety of reasons. At the macro scale the amount of built-up land area is a major concern, as are the distribution of settlements and population. These distributions are also important in relation to other resources such as amenity areas, open countryside and resources generally. At the meso or 'city' scale, form in all its aspects plays a major role in both expediting and impeding urban functions and activities in general, as well as choices and opportunities at the individual level. As Lynch has put it: 'The pattern of urban development critically affects a surprising number of problems, by reason of the spacing of buildings, the location of activities, the disposition of lines of circulation' (Lynch 1961 p 79). Among the things so influenced by urban form are the distribution of employment opportunities, shops, entertainment, open space, and other people, and accessibility to all of these. Certain forms can inhibit interaction and diminish accessibility, whilst others can do just the reverse. Some forms have higher potentialities for growth, change and adaptation than do others, and some offer greater possibilities for choice and participation. These points will be considered later in more detail.

Finally, at the micro level the dispositions, type and groupings of buildings are of importance in the movement patterns they encourage or discourage; in the energy they require to keep them running; in their possibilities for adaptation and change; and in the perceptual and aesthetic stimulation they offer – a factor also to be considered at the meso level of the city as a whole.

The question of the influence of environment upon behaviour is important both at the micro and the meso level. Whilst not wishing to advocate a philosophy of environmental determinism, environment clearly exerts an influence upon behaviour in many ways. Such influences range from the time and distance it takes to get from one place to another with the corresponding encouragement and discouragement of certain journeys, the influence exercised by layouts on social interaction (see Units 6, 7 and 29) and the constraints on certain groups imposed by the distribution of facilities in the city as a whole.

Dr René Dubos argues that:

... the body and the mind are *shaped* by the adaptive responses that man makes to the physicochemical, social, behavioural and even historical stimuli they impinge on him ... Man makes himself in the very act of responding to his environment – through an uninterrupted series of feedback processes ... For this reason, environmental planning plays a key role in enabling human beings to actualize their potentialities. Human potentialities, whether physical or mental, can be realized only to the extent that circumstances are favourable to their existential manifestations. (Dubos 1972 p 178)

In the long term, of course, the influence is reciprocal in that the built environment changes and grows in response to man's preferences and activities and the demands he makes. Indeed Alexander (1970) has argued that the important question is *not* whether environment influences behaviour, but whether (and how far) it satisfies social and cultural demands. If environment or urban form does not wholly meet our requirements then changes are clearly necessary. Frequently, however, such changes require social and political changes, and this points to one major limitation of changes in the urban form. Although many social problems have physical or spatial manifestations, changes in the physical environment *alone* will achieve little. Poverty cannot be rectified by rehousing the poor in clean, new, bright, spacious estates. This merely transfers the problem of poverty from one area to another. Thus, we must ensure that our concern with the physical problems of the city 'for which we can at least see concrete, albeit expensive, solutions' (White 1969 p 15) does not mask more important problems. We must try, in White's words, to treat 'the causes of the urban dilemma rather than just the symptoms'. We must beware of what Reinholt Niehbur has termed 'salvation through bricks'.

Notwithstanding the above mentioned points, environmental factors such as type and quality of housing, access to employment, open space provision and the like, combine with earned income to form what Harvey (1971) terms 'real income'. Concern for urban form and the satisfaction of social demands upon the urban environment must, therefore, entail a concern for the *distribution* of such environmental components of real income, as well as with their totality and overall performance. In other words, rather than working on the criterion of *allocational efficiency* or *pareto optimality* (which states that efficiency exists when no one can be made better off without someone else being made worse off), we must add the criterion of *distributional efficiency*.

I am far from convinced, however, that redistributive physical planning can exert much influence overall. Apart from monetary income being the major consideration, many urban facilities such as area, house type, etc. are distributed on the criterion of ability to pay. Thus, once again the burden of change is seen to lie at the national political level.

Even accepting these caveats it is still necessary to attempt to detail the demands that are, or should be, made of urban form even if the fulfilment of some of these demands is dependent upon the political process. Lynch has argued that we must begin by:

... evaluating the range of possible alternatives of form, on the arbitrary assumption that the metropolis can be moulded as desired. For it is as necessary to learn what is desirable as to study what is possible; realistic action without purpose can be as useless as idealism without power. Even the range of what is possible may sometimes be extended by fresh knowledge of what is desirable. (Lynch 1961 p 79)

Some recent authors have come to the conclusion that a concern with form *per se* is an irrelevancy, based on outmoded conceptions of what cities ought to be like rather than on a concern with social processes and urban functions. Melvin Webber forcefully expressed this view:

... I contend that we have been searching for the wrong grail, that the values associated with the desired urban structure do not reside in spatial structure *per se*. One pattern of settlement and its internal land use form is superior to another only as it better serves to accommodate on-going social processes and to further the non-spatial ends of the political community. I am flatly rejecting the contention that there is an overriding universal spatial or physical aesthetic of urban form. (Webber 1963 p 52)

I would agree with Webber in rejecting any one universal aesthetic of urban form, for on the one hand this would neglect the role of cultural and historical differences between and within different countries, and on the other hand it would be a totally static notion, which failed to understand and accept the impossibility and undesirability of 'final forms' in a changing and developing world. 'To predict an ultimate form, is to commit the historic blunder of monolithic, idealistic end-planning. It leaves out of account society and its changing values' (Jones 1971). Though there may be no overriding universal spatial or physical aesthetic of urban form, this is not to say, however, that there is no aesthetic whatsoever. The great weakness of the 'form follows function' urban theorists is that all too often the functions suggested as important are very partial. The city is not purely the product of communications. It also fulfils – or should do – a variety of social and psychological functions, though these are all too often neglected. In rejecting the historically over dominant role of visual aesthetics in urban design it is vital that the baby is not thrown out with the bathwater. Though urban form must allow, and indeed encourage, the efficient functioning of the city, the city is also the home of man, and as such should be a pleasing place to live in.

SAQ 1   Define the terms 'micro', 'meso', and 'macro' as they are used in the unit.

SAQ 2   Why is urban form important?

SAQ 3   Distinguish the terms *allocational efficiency* and *distributional efficiency*.

SAQ 4   If there is no overriding universal spatial or physical aesthetic of urban form, does this imply that there is no aesthetic whatsoever?

2 Criteria for urban form

Quite clearly, if there are three different scales of urban form – macro, meso and micro – we cannot assume that the criteria necessary for assessing form at these scales will be similar. Hence we must attempt to formulate three different sets of criteria. As the meso level of city structure has been the subject of most work in this area we shall consider it first and in most detail. It should be noted, however, that the selection of criteria inevitably involves us in value judgements and normative procedures, especially if we try to rank criteria in order of preference or importance. This is so because we are not engaged in the more neutral task of describing and analysing urban forms, but are trying to outline what should be. Albers' distinction between two different meanings of the term 'theory' is illustrative in this context:

... It may mean a theory of the forces shaping reality, concerning itself with the observation of an existing structure understood as an object of empirical research; and it may mean a theory of how to form structure by the instruments of planning, considering structure as the object – and the outcome – of planning synthesis. Thus, we have to distinguish between the descriptive and the normative approach to urban structure, between the analysis of an actual and the construction of a desirable or even optimal pattern of spatial distribution. (Albers 1968 p 14)

Given the inevitability of value judgements, how do we go about selecting and formulating criteria for urban form? Perhaps the most sensible first step is to specify some of the elements that together constitute urban form. We can then attempt to suggest certain basic criteria for both the individual and the more abstract concept of city organization and functioning.

2.1 The elements of urban form

Various authors, notably Wurster, Albers, and Lynch, have suggested a variety of classifications of the elements of urban form and their dominant characteristics as a basis for the classification of urban form. In that all are basically concerned with the density, size and arrangement of elements within the urban structure, they all draw, to a greater or lesser extent, upon the pioneering work of Lynch and Rodwin (1958). These two writers distinguished at the most basic level between what they termed 'adapted spaces', that is areas which are adapted to accommodate more or less specified human activities, and 'flow systems', that is systems whose purpose is to allow a flow of persons, goods or services between such areas. This twofold grouping is, however, so basic and general as to be of little practical use. More specifically, Lynch has distinguished three vital elements over and above that of size. These are 1 structural density and condition; 2 the capacity, type and pattern of circulation facilities; 3 the location of large fixed activities.

Lynch goes on to argue that:

... When we come to analyse any one of these three elements of spatial pattern, we find that the most significant features of such patterns are the *grain* (the degree of intimacy with which the various elements such as stores and residences are related), the *focal organization* (the interrelation of the nodes of concentration and interchange as contrasted with the general background), and the *accessibility* (the general proximity in terms of time of all points in the region to a given kind of activity or facility). (Lynch 1961 p 80)

Before considering the more general criteria relating to combinations of elements and the urban form as a whole, let us examine three elements in particular which are often considered crucial: density, size and grain. The first point to note is that the first two elements cannot be treated as completely separate. The population density of some cities in earlier centuries reputedly reached between 100 and 300 persons per hectare, as compared to the 40 per

Figure 1 The question of scale: the intersection of the Santa Monica and San Diego Freeways
Source: California Department of Transportation.

hectare of contemporary New York and 12 per hectare of Los Angeles. The
scale, however, has completely changed (see Figure 1). A city of one
square mile at a density of 200 pph surrounded by open countryside is very
different from a city of say 1,000 square miles at a density of 40 pph.
Changes in dimensions create changes in the properties of the object. What may have been
tolerable densities at one scale, may be very different at another.

. . . Density is only one, limited and mechanistic measure of community life . . . If
varying atomic weights were given to their degree of encumbrance of the land, the
western city would have a much higher density than cities of the past. (Delos Three
1972)

Just as density and size are intimately related – at least where the experience
of living is concerned, so too various writers (Delos Three Symposium on
'Living at High Densities') have stated that density cannot be separated from
the technological level of society, especially transportation. As developments
in transport technology have allowed the spread of urban settlements over
wider areas than ever before, so they have, at certain hours and in certain
areas, brought thousands or millions of people back to the centre, creating
extremely high densities both en route and at destination. Similarly, density
should not be considered independently of culture for 'culture is probably
the most significant variable in determining what constitutes a stressful density'
(Delos Three 1972 p 214, also see Unit 6). Finally, we should not forget the
factor of wealth. Low income families and high income families might live at
high densities, but their life styles will differ considerably. The high income
families for instance, may possess a weekend retreat in the country. We may
confidently agree with one of the conclusions of the Delos Three Symposium
on 'Living at High Densities' namely: 'The same quantitative densities do not
necessarily result in the same qualitative ones.'

Notwithstanding this conclusion, density is far from unimportant. Densities of various dimensions can promote or interfere with the attainment of different sorts of human values. Although cultural and other factors act as intermediaries between life and density, there are probably certain density maxima which should not be exceeded under any circumstances. Only above these levels can density be said to be positively detrimental. Otherwise, density can and does exert clearly positive functions such as social cohesion, security and contact. What are clearly needed are different ranges of densities and, very importantly, the possibility of effective choice between them.

The question of density apart, it is apparent that many urban residents step 'from their front door straight into the impersonal faceless city with no "human scale" intermediary'. It can be argued, however, that 'a hierarchy of spatial experiences is as necessary in human settlements as in biological and ecological phenomena' (Bell and Tyrwhitt 1972 p 237). If this is true then man's immediate environment should act as an interface between his personal interests and the larger urban structure. In effect this is an argument for urban villages or neighbourhoods of one type or another (see Unit 7). These need not necessarily be planned. What is necessary is that they exist. Indeed, in that planned neighbourhoods are frequently so over-simplified as to be sterile, it could well be that organic unplanned neighbourhoods are necessary.

'Simplification' brings up the consideration of 'grain' and the associated planning postulate of zoning or land use segregation. The segregation of industry from residential areas started in Britain in the late nineteenth century as a necessary counter measure to the ill-health and disease engendered by the huddling together of factories and homes in the industrial revolution. I would argue that now, however, the practice continues even when the generating causes have vanished. Modern planning practice separates virtually every activity into discrete areas. The end result is a coarse grained land use pattern which brings in its wake a lack of variety and activity as well as increased journey times to various land uses such as shops and offices.

2.2 General criteria

The variables discussed above, ie density, scale and grain are all distinct, physical elements of urban form and as such can yield concrete criteria. There are, however, many other more abstract higher level less directly physical criteria such as freedom and choice. Lynch, for example, distinguishes the criteria of choice and interaction as the two most important.

> . . . As far as possible, the individual should have the greatest variety of goods, services, and facilities readily accessible to him. He should be able to choose the kind of habitat he prefers; he should be able to enter many kinds of environment at will including the control over his world. These advantages appear in an environment of great variety and fine grain, one in which transportation and communication are as quick and effortless as possible. (Lynch 1961 p 92)

On the subject of interaction, Lynch states that:

> . . . potential interaction between people should be as high as possible, as long as the individual can control it and shield himself whenever desired. His front door, figuratively speaking, should open on to a bustling square, and his back door on a secluded park. Thus this ideal is seen as related to the ideal of choice. (Lynch 1961 p 93)

Other objectives Lynch mentions are those of minimum capital cost and minimum operating cost, and comfort and individual participation. Of the many aesthetic and psychological goals which the city should satisfy, Lynch believes that the most clear cut is that the city should be 'imageable', 'that is, it should be visually vivid and well-structured; its component parts should be easily recognized and easily interrelated. This objective would encourage the use of intensive centres, variety, sharp grain (clear outlines between parts), and a differentiated but well-patterned flow system.' (Lynch 1961 p 94)

Leaving aside objectives such as the health or safety of the environment which Lynch feels cannot be said to be attributes of any specific type of form, he concludes with the goal of adaptability to changing demands and circumstances.

Albers (1968) has also suggested three basic criteria for urban form, which closely parallel Lynch's three criteria of adaptability, choice and variety. They are, respectively:

1 Growth and change shall be possible with respect to the overall structure as well as to the different elements.
2 The locational relations of various 'adapted spaces' should allow a wide variation of choices with respect to basic human activities.
3 Individuation and differentiation of elements in the overall structure should not only be allowed but promoted. (Albers 1968 p 18)

You may have noticed that few of the criteria mentioned above were economic in nature. Indeed, economic considerations tend to enter into the equation more as constraints rather than as criteria. This is as it should be in that a consideration of man and his needs is the preface to a consideration of the types of space necessary for a human environment, and the costs thereof. Constantine Doxiades has outlined why:

... Up to now measurements in cities have been based on economic criteria, but these define feasibility more than goals ... Man's most precious commodity ... is his own life ... This is the basic commodity ... upon which our formula for the city will have to be based. (Doxiades 1972 p 160)

Leonard Duhl has expressed much the same sentiments:

... human, psychological, and social values still follow as afterthoughts, like icing on the planning cake ... (whereas there is) ... a powerful case for psycho-social values transcending all other considerations in the planning of urban space and its physical environment. (Duhl 1963 p 136)

The importance of psychological criteria is equally relevant at the micro level, where we are concerned with individual buildings, groups of buildings, and their associated spaces and layouts. In other words our concern is largely architectural, and hence with the real or perceived satisfaction derived by both the occupants and passers-by from the individual buildings and their collective arrangements. This is not to say that design related economic criteria are unimportant, but apart from the criteria advanced by Stone and Stein and discussed in Unit 30, economic considerations do generally serve as constraints rather than as criteria.

Perhaps the most important psychological criteria at the micro scale is that the built environment be visually stimulating. This quality is not absolute and differs between individuals and cultures (Rapoport and Hawkes 1970). We can say, however, that visual stimulation lies roughly midway between the opposite poles of monotony and sensory or perceptual overload, ie there is an optimum level of perceptual input. This level of stimulation is, it is frequently argued, necessary for the healthy functioning of the individual, and its components are held to be *complexity* and *ambiguity*, that is intricate design capable of a variety of interpretations; a multiplicity of meanings. Rapoport and Kanter (1967) operationalize these qualities as 'detectable variations within an established system of expectations', pointing out that a totally predictable environment is a totally unstimulating one in terms of the usable information offered.

At the macro level of urban form, ie that of the city region and larger aggregations, three criteria in particular would seem to be of importance. First a high level of accessibility within the area as a whole, secondly a degree of differentiation, functional and otherwise, in order to avoid an excessive homogeneity of environment, and finally and most importantly, the preservation of open countryside and access to it. In effect this means some separation of urban areas and the prevention of coalescence. It is worth noting in this context that Toynbee (1972) sees the role of the town dweller as having temporarily changed from the prisoner of the city of yesteryear to the conqueror of the countryside today. He views this as only temporary, however, in that as man conquers the countryside, he transforms it and annexes it to the city. His ominous conclusion is that:

... when all the dry land on the face of our planet has been annexed to the city in one way or another, the city dweller is going to become, once again, the prisoner that he once was in the nineteenth century; and this time there will be no escape for him by any further improvement in his means of communication. (Toynbee 1972 p 86)

The crucial phrase is, of course, 'in one way or another', for in one sense much of the dry land on the planet has already been annexed to the city through the growing domination of urban organization. In Webber's phrase the city has become society. In another, more purely physical sense, a total annexation is still a very long way off, if we mean the conversion of all land to urban uses. As the figures for England and Wales presented in Unit 30 showed, only fifteen per cent at most of the land area is likely to be urbanized by the year 2000. In the US the figure is only four per cent. Thus, though our cities are

Figure 2 Predicted growth of traffic in the Lake District: 1964–2010   Source: *New Society* (1961)

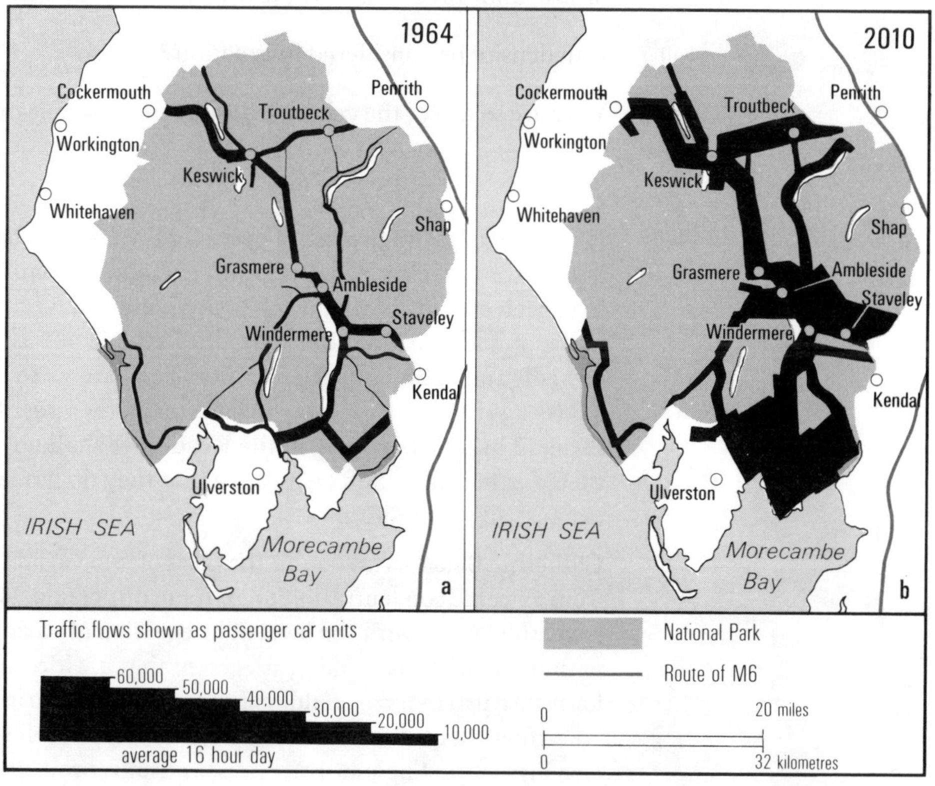

steadily growing in extent, and though access to open space is clearly going to become more of a problem, especially for those who either do not own a car or are too poor to afford a lengthy journey by public transport, the future envisaged by Toynbee is still a long way off. What is much more imminent is the more intensive use of the open space and recreational areas we do have. For example, the number of visitors' journeys to the Lake District increased almost twofold between 1960 and 1970, from an average of 3,300 journeys per day to an average of 5,900 (White 1971). At this rate of increase, the National Parks roads would be saturated by the end of the century if nothing were done (see Figures 2a and 2b).

To sum up, the great bulk of the criteria that have been advanced for the evaluation of urban form has been at the meso or city scale. These range from the more purely physical criteria of density, scale, locality and grain, to more abstract social and psychological criteria. There were few actual economic criteria apart from those of cost minimization, as economic considerations usually function as constraints. In addition, it is right and proper to state what we desire first, and then cost its feasibility, rather than allowing cost considerations to dictate our choice in the first instance. At the micro scale many of the same points apply, but the main criterion was stated to be that of perceptual satisfaction. Finally, it was argued that at the macro scale of urban development, ie the scale of the larger settlement patterns, the criteria of accessibility, differentiation and the preservation of the countryside, were of importance. However, the selection of criteria is inevitably a subjective process and you may or may not agree with those put forward by myself and other authors. It is imperative, however, to have some criteria – however debatable – in order to evaluate the potentials of different forms.

SAQ 5 Is it possible to distinguish neutral criteria for urban form?

SAQ 6 Lynch distinguished three factors relevant to urban form over and above that of size, and three significant features of such forms. What were they?

SAQ 7 Can density be considered in isolation?

SAQ 8 Why are so few of the criteria considered economic ones?

3 Classification of future urban forms

If we wish to avoid the risk of 'freezing the forms of life prematurely and irrevocably' (Keller 1972) we must examine as many possibilities as we are able to conceive of, evaluating each of them in terms of the criteria advanced in the previous section. Lynch delineated five possibilities on the basis of grain, focal organization, and accessibility. They are 1 the dispersed sheet; 2 the galaxy; 3 the core city; 4 the urban star; 5 the ring. As these forms are described in detail in Lynch's paper in the Reader we shall not attempt to describe them further here. Suffice it to say that they do not, as Lynch himself recognized, exhaust all possibilities.

Catherine Bauer Wurster, on the basis of two variables (a form variable ranging from extreme concentration to extreme dispersion, and a scale variable concerned more with the level of integration of various activities and functions within the urban complex), suggested that a wide range of hypothetical choices for future urban form could be generated if the variables were taken as co-ordinate axes. Four of these in particular she felt were likely possibilities (see Figure 3). These were: 1 present trends projected, ie the dispersal of most functions such as shops and residences and industry with certain functions, such as decision making, being even more concentrated in the central cities; 2 general dispersion; 3 concentrated super city; 4 a constellation of relatively diversified and integrated cities – noting of the latter that 'with cities of differing size and character a range from moderate dispersion to moderate concentration would be feasible' (Wurster 1963 p 78). Clearly, Wurster's dispersed city and her concentrated city parallel Lynch's first and third possibilities. The projection of present trends and the constellation are, however, fresh possibilities.

Figure 3 Wurster's four possibilities for urban development
Source: Wurster (1963)

Figure 4 Albers' classification of urban form
Source: Albers (1968)

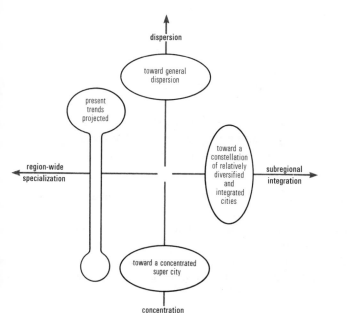

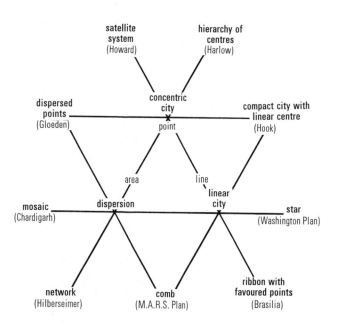

None of the foregoing represent planned possibilities though, and the ranges of alternatives are both partial and not wholly systematic. Albers' classification is thus of value. Although more purely geometrical in origin, Albers bases his classification upon the concentric satellite idea of Howard, the linear idea of Soria-y-Mata and the idea of dispersal propounded by Frank Lloyd Wright in his Broadacre City, ie point, line and area.

... It seems possible to derive the great majority of proposals for urban structure advocated in the course of our century from the differentiation and combination of these three basic elements; concentric city, linear city, and uniformly dispersed settlement structure. (Albers 1968, see Figure 4)

Almost all of the possibilities listed above are related to the meso scale of individual city structure. Perhaps the sole exception is Wurster's idea of a constellation of cities. That this is so is, I would suggest, a result of the pace of urban development which has been so rapid that urban theory has lagged far behind urban reality in certain areas, notably in this sphere of urban growth, urban influence and urban coalescence. As yet theorists are still at the stage of trying to grasp conceptually what is happening, let alone suggesting possibilities and strategies for future development. As such these various conceptualizations are discussed in Section 7.

At the micro level, future possibilities are conceived largely in terms of the flexibility and adaptability of constituent elements, ie in terms of 'plug-in' architecture, modular building techniques and 'instant' housing. Thus possibilities at this level are generally of a technical rather than theoretical nature, though such possibilities clearly have implications at the meso level. In a sense this is only to be expected as it is simultaneously less important and more difficult to conceptualize alternative forms at the micro level, not least because they are not confined largely to pattern. In addition developments at this scale can be left to look after themselves much more on the grounds of both freedom of expression and of the perceptual variety likely to result.

SAQ 9   On what basis did Wurster formulate her classification of possible forms?

SAQ 10   Which three elements does Albers believe underlie most proposals for urban structure this century?

4 Evaluation of future urban forms

Before attempting to evaluate the various possible forms outlined above, we should note that it is not only the criteria for evaluation which are non-neutral. Albers has expressed the view that various structural proposals frequently have more to them than their advocacy of different geometrical elements. They are often the manifestations of more fundamental social or economic values.

. . . It is the fear of over concentration and of social and economic disadvantages which has done much to nourish the idea of decentralization to which both the linear development and the dispersal offer theoretical solutions. The idea of a dispersed structure owes much to the socio-cultural idea of overcoming the tensions between town and country and is based at the same time on the notion of technological progress implying ubiquitous availability of energy and communications services. (Albers 1968 p 18)

Jane Jacobs has said of Ebenezer Howard that 'he not only hated the wrongs and mistakes of the city, he hated the city and thought it an outright evil and an affront to nature that so many people should get themselves into an agglomeration. His prescription for saving the people was to do the city in' (Jacobs 1972 p 27). Jacobs herself, however, writes from an equally value-laden viewpoint, that of a committed urbanist.

Without evaluating every single form in terms of every criteria, let us proceed to examine some of them, taking first the polar extremes, the concentrated city and the dispersed city. The concentrated city has the advantage that accessibility should, theoretically, be high, the higher densities permitting fully utilized public systems. It should also be more 'imageable' (in Lynch's terminology) as well as having a higher degree of community feeling and a wide choice of activities. Economically it should also have lower running costs assuming scale economies still operate. On the negative side it could be relatively uncomfortable, there might be a poor individual range of housing types, and individual participation might be more doubtful. Flexibility and adaptability would be very low, and expansion difficult. Albers notes in this context that there is an inevitable conflict between our attempts to give form to our environment, and the knowledge that form serves needs, and that needs are likely to change. Wurster views the development of such concentrated supercities as highly unlikely, except under very special conditions.

Low density dispersal, on the other hand, is extremely flexible and adaptable, though difficult to control as regards such growth and change. It also allows local participation and can produce a certain type of environmental satisfaction. It is extremely expensive however, both in terms of facility provision, land consumption and time-distance costs. It has relatively poor accessibility, and choice of activities and facilities are also poor. Its imageability is very low. Wurster believes that residential development in such a form would probably 'take the form of socially specialized enclaves . . . with class and race conflicts' (Wurster 1963 p 97). She further notes that this pattern of development is 'hardly possible in regions with highly concentrated populations where metropolitan areas are already beginning to overlap'. Thus extensive *low density* dispersal is as generally unlikely as high density, high rise supercities.

Lynch's 'urban galaxy' is a type of concentrated dispersion, development being 'bunched into relatively small units, each with an internal peak of density'. A compromise alternative, it possesses both the advantages and the disadvantages of compromises. Accessibility would be higher, as would the availability of activities and facilities, but overall choice – of friends, employment, etc – could remain relatively low, especially if the clusters were fairly widely separated. Also, as Lynch notes, 'flexibility might be lost, since local clusters would of necessity have relatively fixed boundaries, if interstitial spaces were preserved, and the city-wide activities would be confined to one kind of location' (Lynch 1961 p 85).

If the degree of separation is increased, and the internal densities raised somewhat we move towards Howard's satellite concept, and Wurster's idea of a constellation of cities. The difference between these two possibilities would seem to be largely one of scale, in that at one end of the scale we have small dormitory satellites, progressing through larger, theoretically self-contained communities to cities in their own right. Paralleling this movement along the continuum, the relative balance of advantages and disadvantages changes. Towards the smaller end of the continuum flexibility and adaptability would be higher, as would community participation and interaction. Choice and variety in all their aspects would be limited, however, whilst just the opposite would apply at the larger end of the spectrum. Regarding accessibility, we should distinguish between inter-centre accessibility and intra-centre mobility. The former would be likely to increase with the size of the centres, whilst the latter would be likely to decrease.

The comments of Bell and Tyrwhitt are of interest on this whole question of size, as they believe that though the sizes advocated over time for satellites has increased in Britain, they have always lagged well behind what was necessary.

. . . New, small-scale, self-contained industrial settlements had been advocated in Britain from the time of Robert Owen, 1816, onward . . . Then, four generations later, in 1946, the New Towns Act gave official sanction to the realization of a concept that was by then obsolete in terms of its scale and ideology in relation to the actual problems of the country at that moment in time . . . However, by 1945 the garden cities of 25–50,000 were becoming to be seen as too small. Only after 1950, however, were figures of 250–500,000 taken seriously . . . But the rate of change is still accelerating . . . A handful of new counter-magnet cities of half a million are likely to make no more impact upon this rapid urban expansion than the early garden cities exerted upon the square miles of interwar suburban sprawl. (Bell and Tyrwhitt 1972 p 30)

Constellations of relatively diversified and integrated cities are likely, in Wurster's opinion, 'if the desire for private space and natural amenity is modified by greater concern for accessibility, diversity, and other traditional urban values' (Wurster 1963 p 99). More specifically:

. . . The old central city might remain quite strong, for region-wide functions and highly specialized facilities, but it would have less employment and a relatively balanced population with mixed densities and dwelling types. There would be far less disruption and dislocation than in the Super-City alternative with a much greater chance to preserve the diversity and historic qualities that make for real urbanity . . . In general, the cities might vary greatly in size and character, and they could either become a fairly close-knit regional network with minimal space between or spread quite far out into a larger region, depending on variable purposes and conditions . . . Except for the extremes of scatteration, concentration, and specialization, this pattern would probably offer the greatest choice in life styles. (Wurster 1963 p 100)

Notwithstanding the putative advantages of the constellation, the linear city is often believed to have much in the way of advantages. It has been said for example that a linear organization (a line has neither shape nor size) is the truest reflection of an open society.

Certainly, the linear city could adapt itself for easier growth, as well as offering high accessibility both to activities, facilities and to open space. Its major deficiencies are its lack of focal organization and a very low sense of identity and community participation. Once the linear city exceeds a certain size, some of its advantages such as accessible variety could fall off and for this reason Albers advocates a combination of linear elements; a system of co-ordinated or centrally focused linear elements such as a star-shaped or a comb-shaped pattern can be expected to serve best the present requirements.

The urban star enables fast radial movement, along with a wide degree of choice and variety, and a coherent image. Adaptability, flexibility and growth potential would be reasonable though not excellent. Over a certain size the possibility of congestion both at the centre and along the radials is strong, and circumferential movement would be far from easy. The corollary of this last point however, is that open space can be more easily preserved between the points of the star. Thus, in this respect the star offers good access to open space. The ring, a variant of the linear form, also potentially offers easy access to open space in that it surrounds, and is surrounded by, countryside. It would require strict legislation to keep the centre unbuilt, however, especially if radial routes transversed the internal open space. These radials would offer a level of accessibility which is theoretically higher than extended linear forms in that the line is bent back upon itself, permitting shorter journeys along the diameters rather than the arc. Unfortunately, the very act of closure which is inherent in the ring, severely limits the growth potential of the ring. It would seem, however, that a broken, extendable U-shaped form would have most advantages of the ring plus the advantage of growth potential along the arms of the U. This suggestion basically entails the convolution of the line; convolution in nature allowing length to be gained whilst preserving other features. Further convolution into a 'sinuous 'city permits even more length. Once lateral roads are added, however, we have merely a variant of the grid or network.

Finally we should mention the projection of present trends which Wurster believes would 'probably tend to magnify the present problems of accessibility, inadequate choice, social and political schisms, and rising costs, particularly for transportation and housing' (Wurster 1963 p 96).

Generally it can be seen that few of the possibilities discussed exist in complete isolation. Most of them are related to one another through the manipulation of their basic principles. Thus the ring represents both the closure of the line and the concentric city minus its core. The star is a combination of the line and the concentric city. The satellite system is but a fragmented star, and the galaxy and the dispersed net are extensions of the satellite idea over more extensive areas. None of the possibilities discussed can really be said to be completely unrelated to each other, all are but permutations and combinations on the three-dimensional continuum of point, line and area.

It would be virtually impossible, certainly in a unit, to attempt to undertake a more detailed cost benefit analysis of the various forms, but certain forms do seem to stand out as meeting more criteria than others, these are the constellation of cities, the star, and the linear city. All three forms have found favour with urban planners, particularly the star (Copenhagen, Stockholm and Washington amongst other cities) but also the linear development (Paris), and the satellite system (London). Although this is in large part a reflection of their relative advantages over other forms, it also surely reflects the fact that these three modes of development entail the least restructuring of the existing urban fabric. Instead, they all allow development from the basis of the existing form in certain specified directions.

Turning briefly to the micro scale, Albers' comments on plug-in cities are worth noting. Referring to the view that the division of cities in separate land use areas is outmoded, and to the belief that the built environment should be highly flexible in order to accommodate changing social processes, he notes that:

. . . The range of possible remedies begins with the re-introduction of dwellings into city centres, . . . and ends up in the vision of an overall framework for a flexible urban structure, a huge scaffolding equipped with all necessary technical services and designed to be filled with prefabricated elements which can be plugged into the system, dismantled and exchanged for other elements if needs require another combination . . . Upon closer inspection such ideas lose something of their fascination. The seeming flexibility of the elements is paid for by a vast advance investment in a framework which in itself is rather inflexible and therefore open to obsolescence; the exchange of such elements holds little promise of being simple and inexpensive, if we may judge from experience with moving movable partitions. Most important, the degree of freedom in such a framework is rapidly diminishing as the structure comes to be filled in and reaches densities which correspond to those in conventional buildings. (Albers 1968 p 18)

It will be evident by now that there is no clear-cut solution to the problem of urban form even with the 'pure' types Lynch describes and evaluates. In actuality the problems are compounded as 'a plan for a metropolis is more likely to be a complex and mixed one, to be realized as an episode in some continuous process, whose form involves rate and direction of change as well as a momentary pattern' (Lynch 1961 p 95). None the less, this should not deter us from attempting to assess different urban structures 'in terms of the set of human ends (or benefits) they will serve, the other ends forgone, and the differing means (or costs) required to achieve these benefits' (Wurster 1963 p 79).

SAQ 11 Attempt to specify the advantages and disadvantages of:
    a low density dispersal;
    b the constellation of cities.

SAQ 12 Which three forms have met with more favour than others and why?

5 March and Martin and the new geometry

Inherent in almost all conceptions of the future urban form are certain structural alternatives. High densities are seen as implying high accessibility, high rise buildings and minimal open space. Low densities, on the other hand, are popularly associated with low accessibility, low rise housing and much more open space. These two parameters have determined thinking about the built form for a long time. The great contribution of March and Martin's work is that it has partially broken through these barriers, revealing many fallacies in the conventional wisdom. As March and Martin (1972) wrote in the introduction to their book *Urban Space and Structures*, 'In most towns which appear to be overcrowded all the land that is needed is there if *the right principles* are used to find it' (my emphasis). More specifically, March has written:

... the notions of concentrated or dispersed developments have no relationship to population density. It is as possible to have a high-density dispersed pattern as a low-density concentrated pattern.

Accessibility requires a higher linear density, but this is not to be confused with a high surface density. Indeed, with ribbon development, high linear densities can be achieved with low surface densities. This is its unique property. (March 1967)

Such assertions are of little use on their own and we must therefore examine the bases of March and Martin's conceptual revolution in more detail. Several principles are involved but a useful starting point is their statement that:

... The question of tall or low buildings is not simply an argument about two alternative building forms. There are in fact points of recognition in a more generalized spectrum in which, as the envelope constantly changes from high to low, and from a tower to its inverse, the hollow square, this in turn gives rise to a series of constantly changing internal relationships and to constantly changing space around the building itself. (March and Martin 1972 p 3)

Martin (1972, see the Reader excerpt) demonstrates that any given grid of streets defines the general plot pattern. To alter the plot pattern it is necessary to alter the grid of streets. He further shows that for any given grid pattern there exists an optimum balance between the plot, the amount of building it can reasonably support, and the street system (or grid) which serves it. If the pressure for floor space increases, as it has done in New York and almost all other major cities, the logical solution is to increase the scale of the grid so that the balance is retained. What in fact has almost always occurred is that the existing grid has exerted a powerful inertial influence, such that the only way of increasing floor space is perceived as being an increase in building height on each plot. As a result the balance between the various elements disappears.

Martin demonstrates the advantages of the court form over the pavilion by utilizing the principle embodied in Fresnel's square (see Figure 5) in which each successive square diminishes in width but has exactly the same area as its predecessor. He shows that the central square and the outer annulus are two possible ways of placing the same amount of floor space on the same site. More specifically, he is able to show that by increasing the size of the grid bounded by Park Avenue and Eighth Avenue, and 42nd and 37th Street in New York, and replacing the existing pavilion-type building by courts, it would be possible to reduce the height of all the buildings by a factor of four whilst providing as much open space as 28 Washington Squares in the area (see Reader for details and diagrams).

Going on to select from the continuous transformation of forms from point to area, just three possibilities, the pavilion or tower, the street and the court, March and Martin state that:

... When the built potential is plotted against the number of storeys for each of the three built forms described, assuming all other factors are constant, then it is seen that after a certain height the tower form ceases to use land with increasing efficiency ...

Figure 5 Fresnel's square Source: March & Martin (1972)

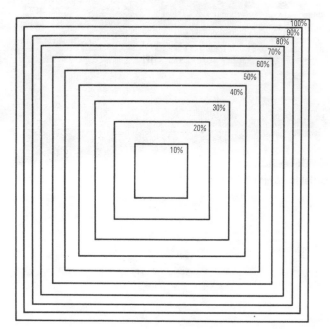

Figure 6 The relative built efficiency of the tower, street and court forms of development Source: March & Martin (1972)

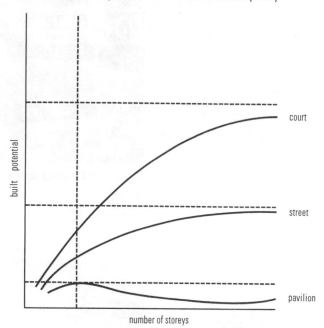

(see Figure 6). This could be one reason that the 'City of Towers', free standing towers in a park-like setting has never been built. It is inherently inefficient in terms of land use. In comparison to the pavilion or tower form at its maximum, the built potential of the street form has twice its value, and the built potential of the court form is no less than three times as great. (March and Martin 1972 pp 35–7)

You should read or refer to Le Corbusier's Plan for a contemporary city (see Reader) in this context.

You will remember from figures quoted in Unit 30 that whereas two million acres of land in Britain were in urban use in 1900, the figure is now four million and six million is the expected figure for the year 2000 *if development continues in its present form*. March (1967), however, has calculated that every household *could* have a house, a garden and a car on two million acres in the year 2000. With favourable land-use planning, ie increasing the scale of the grid and by building in courts, March asserts that semi-detached houses can be built at 200 people to the acre and three-storey terraces at up to 265 people to the acre. The conventional confusion between residential building forms and density stems almost entirely from conventional notions of scale, and a tendency as March puts it to think in blobs, rather than lines. Examples of these possibilities are examined in the TV programmes associated with this block. Also part of the Eastfields project is illustrated in Figure 7, and part of the Pollards Hill project (both in the London borough of Merton) in Figures 8 and 9. The layout of the Pollards Hill project shown in Figure 8 embodies two other principles worthy of discussion. Though perimeters may be lengthened by building in a linear fashion around open space, they can be increased even more by convolution. Figures 10a, 10b, 10c and 10d indicate how it is possible to convolute a line of housing in three different ways in order to gain, respectively, about 1.5, 2 and 3 times the straight length (March 1972). The fourth of these techniques was used in the Pollards Hill project. Clearly the size of gardens (or private open space) is limited by convolution, though public open space may remain considerable. At Eastfields, for example, the public open space is some 3 hectares (7.5 acres) in extent – all enclosed by

Figure 7 An individual square at Eastfields   Photo: S. W. Newberry

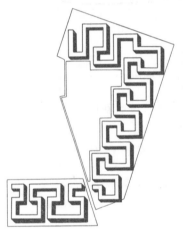

Figure 8   The Grecian frieze pattern of Pollards Hill Source: March (1972)

Figure 9 Pollards Hill from the road Photo: S. W. Newberry

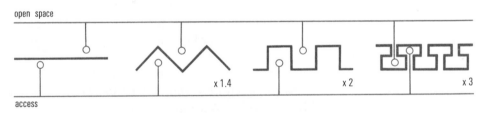

Figure 10 The convolution of a line to gain length   Source: March (1972)

housing, all roads and garages being around the external perimeter of the development.

The question of gardens raises the point made by March (1967) that 'density is essentially a matter of how much or how little private open space a household is to have'. This does not necessarily mean, however, that high densities can only be bought at the price of minimal private space. Even in March's calculations concerning placing the entire population of this country on two million acres in the year 2000 he assumed a minimum plot size of 20 feet by 100 feet. He does show, however, that a *small* reduction in the size of garden enables a marked change in density.

Figure 11 Court development around a village green

Quite clearly the whole question of density and layout is a two-edged sword. Though the absolute saving in land from higher densities falls off quite rapidly (see Unit 30) thus knocking away the theoretical props for many high density central area redevelopments, it is possible to develop low rise high density dwellings. Thus, March and Martin's findings enable the development of either high density low rise concentrated centres with plenty of open space or high density *dispersed* settlement. March himself believes that though the demonstration of the possibility of high density low rise concentrated housing clarifies the principles involved, we would be better off encouraging high density dispersed development. 'Instead of permitting the highest densities in the countryside where they can make the greatest sense, we insist on putting the highest density towards the centres of our cities' (March 1967).

March bases this argument on the fact that many people would prefer to live in the country if they had high accessibility to city centres, but that our present mode of development is extremely space consuming. It is low density dispersal. By building in a court fashion akin to the housing around old village greens (see Figure 11), March believes that we could have semi-detached rural living at 200 people to the acre. If this were possible, as March argues it is, then there would be no need for high density building in cities in an effort to halt the spread of built-up areas over agricultural land. This idea represents the' continuation of the 'Let's build in lines' idea into the countryside, developing small pieces of land along rural roads here, there and everywhere. This explains March's advocacy of planned ribbon development (not to be confused with low density sprawl, a concept which is anathema to most planners). However, March calculates that linear development gives better access to the countryside than either nucleation or dispersion. Similarly, he maintains that linear development would convey the *subjective impression* of being less built-up, if routes were arranged to cut through the open countryside. If March is correct, this is extremely important in that the visual distinctiveness and separation of town and country is one of the keystones for the conventional arguments in favour of concentrated settlements.

Figure 12 'String-of-beads' development

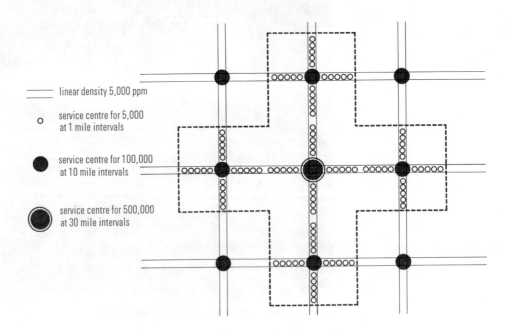

linear density 5,000 ppm

○   service centre for 5,000
    at 1 mile intervals

●   service centre for 100,000
    at 10 mile intervals

◉   service centre for 500,000
    at 30 mile intervals

Returning to March's dictum that with ribbon development high linear densities, and hence high accessibility can be achieved with low surface densities he suggests what might be termed 'string-of-beads' development (see Figure 12).

. . . Suppose a linear density along the route of 5,000 persons per mile . . . then at one mile intervals there would be functions to support 5,000 persons . . . Within ten minutes by bus or five minutes by car there would be facilities to serve 100,000 persons. In a quarter of an hour by car or thirty minutes by bus a regional centre for 500,000.
. . . I believe there are many excellent geometrical reasons . . . to suppose that a free, loose development along a network of routes has advantages of capacity, accessibility, density and use distribution not possible in nuclear development and that, with a positive policy towards open spaces, it is likely to prove the most reasonable form for the emergent city. (March 1967)

The sort of development suggested by March for concentrated settlements is not particularly contentious, being more in the way of a purely technical innovation. Where March's suggestions for high density linear development in the countryside is concerned, the issues become more clouded by value-orientations. March himself tends more towards the mobility and dispersal school of thought, and in this sense is far from being an urbanist in orientation. Although he claims that rural ribbon development will give a greater subjective feeling of open countryside I remain to be fully convinced. His arguments are extremely plausible but his rejection of the desirability of a more or less marked rural-urban dichotomy is somewhat disturbing, even though this judgement reflects no more than a deeply engrained value-orientation which may be quite outmoded.

SAQ 13   What principle is embodied in Fresnel's square?

SAQ 14   When compared to the tower form at its maximum, what are the built potentials of the street form and the court form?

SAQ 15   What reasons does Lionel March give for his advocacy of high density linear development in the countryside?

6 The future urban form and its evolution: urban growth

The most dominant characteristic of almost all contemporary cities is their continued growth – both upwards and, even more importantly, outwards (see Figures 13 and 14). In the case of America, for instance, Bochert records that: 'Four-fifths of the national population increase during the past decade took place within standard metropolitan areas, and virtually all of the increase occurred within metropolitan commuter fields' (Bochert 1972 p 370). Jerome Pickard (1970) has undertaken to place urban growth in America in the matrix of population growth generally. He shows that though the population of the United States reached 100 million in 1915 and 200 million in 1967, ie a doubling period of some 52 years, this doubling period was much shorter in the early days of the Republic. This lengthening of the doubling period is, of course, directly related to a reduction in the annual population growth rate which, although averaging some three per cent per year in the pre-Civil War period, is now down to just over one per cent. Even allowing for the fact that with increasing urbanization, there is some diminution of population growth rates, Pickard projects a population of 300 million by the year 2000, give or take a few millions, and barring unforeseen catastrophe.

This continuing population increase has not been distributed equally, however, and the dominance of the north-eastern area has diminished relatively. Dividing

Figure 13 The outward growth of Los Angeles Source: Mary Banham (1971)

1850, population 2,500

1893, population 160,000

1915–16, population 1,000,000

1932–3, population 3,500,000

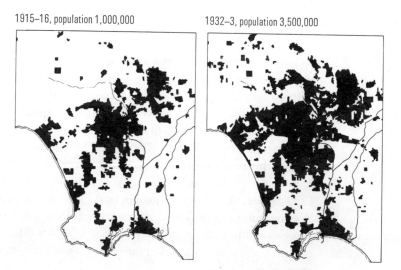

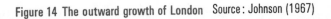

Figure 14 The outward growth of London   Source: Johnson (1967)

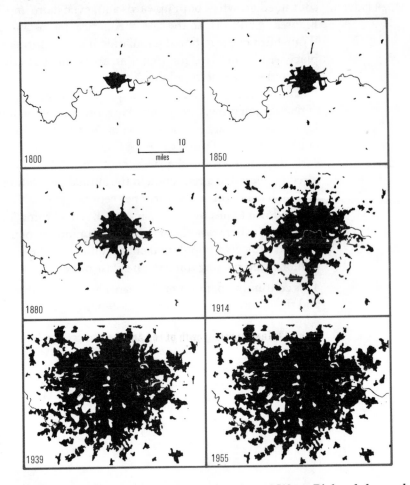

the USA into three areas, North, South and West, Pickard shows that in 1900 the North had 62 per cent of the national population, the South 32 per cent, and the West only 6 per cent. By 1968 these proportions had changed to 52, 31 and 17 per cent respectively – and this out of a more than doubled population. Projecting present trends to the year 2000, Pickard foresees the West advancing to 22 per cent of the total, the South dipping slightly to 26 per cent, and the North holding at 52 per cent. It must be stressed that these changes are relative. Absolutely, the North received one-half of the total population increase in the period 1920–70. The magnitude of the relative change may be measured by the fact that the West's population increased from 28 to 35 million over the decade 1960–70, and an increase to 68 million is predicted for the year 2000.

Relating these changes back to the urban context, Pickard projects increases in population for *all* urban regions, although the interstitial areas have zones of both population increase and decrease. Pickard's most striking projection is, without doubt, that the twelve major urban regions will account for approximately 85 per cent of the entire *net* increase in the nation. The great northern metropolitan belt is projected to increase its population by some 40 million during this period, though the southern urban regions are projected to grow even faster and the western ones faster still. Seven metropolitan areas: Los Angeles, New York, Chicago, San Francisco Bay, Detroit, Miami and Washington have projected increases of at least 3 million each – in the Los Angeles complex the projected increase is 11.6 million. If present trends continue, these seven areas alone will account for over *one-third* of net population growth (see Figure 15).

Figure 15 The twelve main future urban regions of the USA in the year 2000. Numbered in order of population size   Source: Pickard (1970)

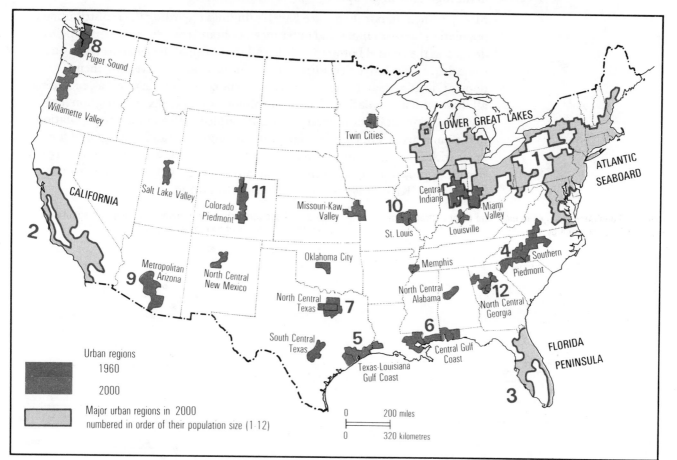

These massive population increases have been paralleled by equally huge increases in the built-up area. Between 1920 and 1970 the seven large urbanized areas which form the cores of the metropolitan growth areas increased their geographic extent from under 2,000 square miles to approximately 9,000 square miles. Over the next thirty years this figure is projected to double to 18,000 square miles, with both Los Angeles and New York projected to have urbanized areas approaching 5,000 square miles each, and Chicago and the San Francisco Bay Area about 2,000 square miles each. As Pickard (1970) comments 'the dimensions of future urban masses are almost unbelievable' (p 6). By way of comparison the Greater London Area has something approaching 700 square miles.

In the United Kingdom, Kivell's analysis of population changes in the 52 English and Welsh metropolitan areas over the period 1961–71 is of interest. He found the general pattern to be one of substantial population growth, with only seven of the areas failing to increase their populations. Of these seven areas, four – London, Liverpool, Manchester and Newcastle – are centred on major conurbations which have severe housing problems. All four have been pursuing active overspill policies. Growth rates over the period varied markedly from near zero to over 30 per cent, and though little correlation was found between size and growth rates, a marked regional distribution of growth rates was found to exist. The South-East in particular emerged as a region of widespread and rapid metropolitan growth, all the metropolitan areas in this region, with the exception of London, having grown faster than the national average. The South-West and the East Midlands were also well represented in the high growth group.

Most pertinent to our theme are Kivell's findings regarding the redistribution of population between inner and outer metropolitan areas, the inner areas being defined as the central boroughs. He found that in 49 of the 52 areas there was some degree of relative decentralization, the outer areas increasing their population at a greater rate than the inner ones. In 27 of the 52 areas, including all those with a population of over one million, absolute decentralization had occurred; growth in the outer areas being coupled with a fall in the population of the inner areas. He suggests that a general tendency can be recognized for areas with more than half a million people to have 'experienced an inner-area decline approaching 10 per cent and an outer area growth of between 10 and 20 per cent' (Kivell 1972 p 181, see Figures 16 and 17).

Figure 16 Population changes in inner and outer metropolitan areas 1961–71, grouped by size Source: Kivell (1972)

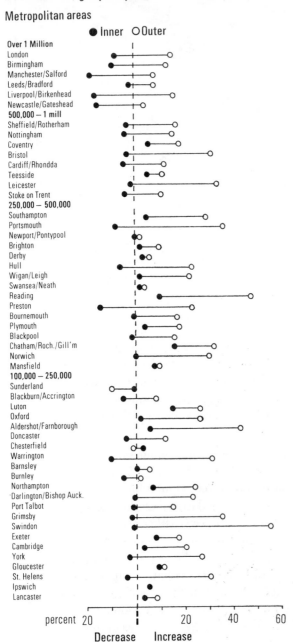

Figure 17 Population changes in inner and outer metropolitan areas 1961–71, grouped by regions Source: Kivell (1972)

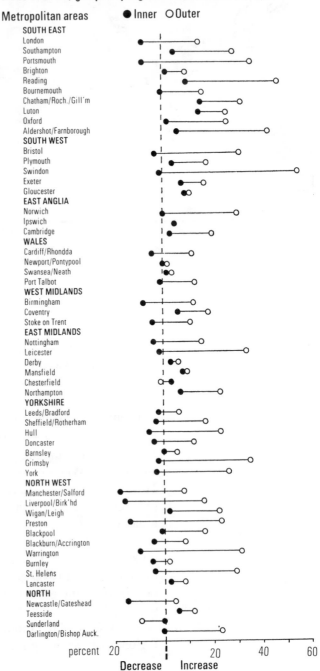

At the macro level of the urban settlement pattern as a whole, March has attempted, using simple models of growth and interregional migration to extrapolate current population changes to the year 2011. He aggregated his data for 1951, 1961 and 1967 into 50 km × 50 km grid squares, 81 of which cover England and Wales. For each cell he took two different growth rates, 1951–61 and 1962–7. We shall consider only the results from the latter as the former are distorted by the rapid growth of London's New Towns over that period. March's results are shown graphically in Figures 18a, 18b and 18c. They show a consolidation of the London-Birmingham-Manchester backbone allied with a dispersal of activities and population within it.

Figure 18a England and Wales with 50–50 km grids superimposed

Figure 18b Population distribution in 1961. Areas which have more than 0.015 of the total population are outlined

Figure 18c Population distribution in 2011 based on 1962–7 trends Source: March (1969)

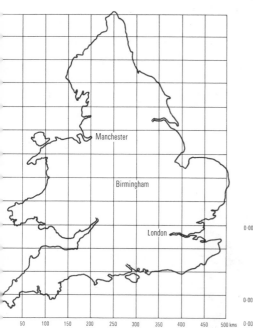

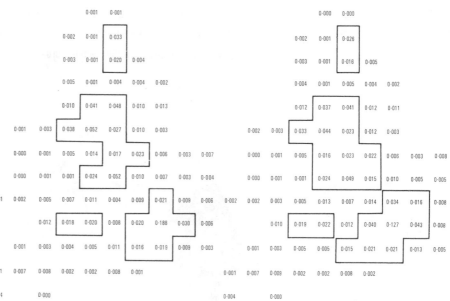

This 'backbone' area occupies about one-third of the land area of England and Wales and currently accounts for about sixty per cent of the population. March sees it as taking up to ninety-five per cent of the growth in population over the fifty year period from 1961 to 2011 and, as a result, concentrating some seventy per cent of the total population by the latter date. March himself recognizes the dangers of this broad-brush extrapolation and comments that it 'inevitably leads to distortion, to statistical fiction rather than fact' (March 1969 p 5). For example, the population projections have recently been revised downwards by the Office of Population Censuses and Surveys. None the less, despite its weaknesses, the approach is valuable for the broad outline it presents. You should note that the findings and projections examined in this section point to the increasing concentration of population within urban regions allied with the decentralization of population within these regions. The next section examines how these two facts and others have been conceptualized in relation to the evolving urban form.

SAQ 16   What do the findings and projections of Bochert, Pickard, Kivell and March have in common?

SAQ 17   What do Pickard's findings indicate in particular, and how do they relate to certain trends outlined in Unit 30?

7 Conceptualizations of the evolving urban form

Facts do not merely present themselves ready ordered to the mind. They have to be structured by man, and it is questionable whether any of the constructions which men place upon facts correspond exactly to the empirical reality of the world we inhabit. Most of them are but the external manifestation of differing value orientations in regard to the organization of space and human activities. All that can be said is that the evidence tends to lend greater support to some constructions than to others. Those who cry for 'the facts and nothing but the facts' pursue a chimera, for selection is inevitable. In periods of relatively slow change certain conceptualizations tend to become dominant and represent man's world view. In periods of rapid change, however, the situation is more fluid and constructions proliferate as men try to make sense of rapidly succeeding situations. It is to these constructions that we now turn (see Figure 19).

Figure 19 Perspectives on the evolving urban form

7.1 Megalopolis

Gottmann coined the term 'megalopolis' to describe that area of the United States that runs from Boston in the north to Washington in the south, taking in New York and Philadelphia. Some 600 miles in length (see Figure 20) it embraced some 30 million people even in 1950. Speaking of its origins, Gottmann (1957 p 189) states that 'It resulted obviously from the coalescence, recently achieved, of a chain of metropolitan areas, each of which grew around a substantial urban nucleus'. It is comprised of 'a continuous stretch of urban and suburban areas' (p 189) and 'extends out on a rapidly growing scale, along highways and rural roads, mixing uses of land that look either rural or urban, encircling vast areas which remain "green"' (p 196). More recently,

Figure 20 Megalopolis on the northeastern Seaboard of the USA Source: Gottmann (1957)

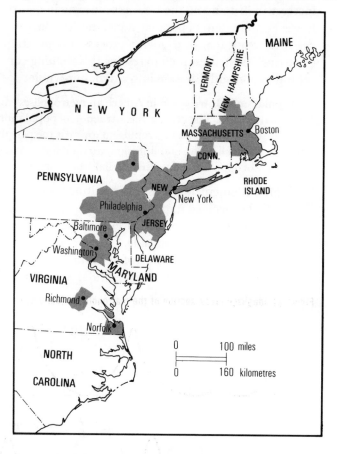

Herman Kahn has foreseen the development of three huge American megalopolises – Boswash (Boston-Washington), Chi-Pitts (Chicago-Pittsburg) and San-San (San Francisco-San Diego).

It is important not to fall into the trap of seeing megalopolis as a continuous built-up urban area such as Greater London or Los Angeles. Gottmann conceptualized the existence of megalopolis in order to distinguish the marked differences between the distinct, separate and clearly bounded towns and cities of yesteryear, and the far larger, more discontinuous and interrelated urban systems of today. Indeed, Robin Best has pointed out that in terms of Gottmann's criteria (density of population and the like), the whole of England and Wales is megalopolitan. It is then, a conceptualization of a change in the scale and extent of the urban settlement pattern in certain parts of the world, rather than a concrete fact. As such it has been severely criticized by some authors.

Freidmann and Miller comment that:

. . . Although later writers have taken it as a generic term for contiguous metropolitan regions, the concept, lacking precision as well as generality, has frequently been misapplied (Freidmann and Miller 1965 p 312)

Keller is even more devastating:

. . . Megalopolis was a tentative notion, a provisional working model . . . All too swiftly, however, it has hardened into an *idée fixe*. The basic questions are being lost sight of as the 'perhaps' becomes the 'will be' . . . Like Babylon, megalopolis now appears to be cropping up everywhere . . . Instead of using the concept as an aid to describe an emerging reality, it is coming to determine that reality. (Keller 1971 p 594)

7.2 The tidal wave As the figures quoted in Section 6 indicate, the great bulk of the population increase in Britain and the USA is occurring in metropolitan regions. Given, however, the extent of popular preference for the suburbs and the associated desire to escape from the cities, a process of population redistribution is occurring. Wolf attempted to resolve this seeming contradiction between centralization and diffusion into a dynamic whole:

... Population redistribution in American metropolises can be interpreted as a dialectical process. The greater the attraction of population to the metropolis – centralization – the greater its repulsion towards the periphery of the metropolis – diffusion. Centralization and diffusion are therefore two sides of the same coin. This 'unity of opposites' constitutes a dialectical process. (Wolf 1969 p 163)

Wolf, after Blumenfeld, likens the resulting spatial pattern to a tidal wave. As Blumenfeld conceived it, population growth rates rise outward from the centre of the metropolis in concentric circular rings until the crest of the wave is reached whereupon they subside. Over time the crest of the wave moves outwards, leaving behind rings of declining growth rates. Figure 21 shows an idealized profile of the metropolitan tidal wave which Wolf divides into four

Figure 21 Idealized cross-section of the metropolitan tidal wave Source: Wolf (1969)

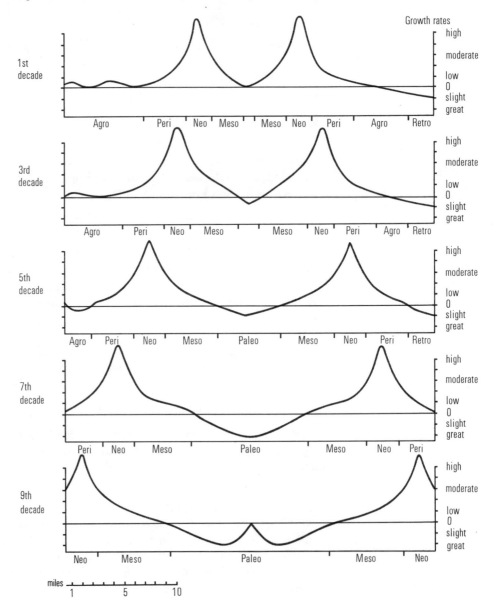

zones. Zone 1, the paleo-urban, comprises the central zone in which population growth rates are negative. Zone 2, the meso-urban is characterized by moderate and diminishing growth rates. Zone 3, the neo-urban, consists of a zone of exceedingly high growth rates, whilst Zone 4, the peri-urban, represents a zone of moderate but increasing growth rates indicative of the approach of the crest.

Wolf applied this concept of the tidal wave to try to predict the likely future distribution of population in the State of Ohio in the year 2000. On the basis of 1960 population statistics and predictions, and on the basis of zones with constant boundaries delimited in 1960 (which of course underestimate the magnitude of the potential changes), Wolf produced the following figures (see Table 1).

Table 1 The tidal wave in Ohio, 1900–2000

	Actual		Forecasted	
	1900	1960	1980	2000
paleo and meso	32.8	39.0	23.2	13.2
neo	8.1	25.1	43.4	48.3
peri	11.5	9.8	12.2	20.5
Total (millions)	52.4	73.9	78.8	81.9

Source: Wolf (1969)

Even though Wolf neglects marked changes in communication which could 'transform the present system', his forecasts seem more realistic for the situation thirty years hence than Berry's forecasts of a total inversion. Wolf suggests that:

... Urban places outside of this complex may stagnate ... (and) ... rural areas beyond the commuter sheds of such of those urban places that continue their growth, will continue to lose population. Indeed, 'empty areas' will become larger and more frequent. (Wolf 1969)

More important than any of the specific figures, however, are the conceptual pegs Wolf's scheme affords us. He emphasizes:

... the permanence of the metropolitan foci as major central points in the redistribution of population, in contrast to the disruption of metropolitan spatial structure so easily inferred from the hypothesis of 'explosion'. (Wolf 1969 p 153)

... The populace is attracted to the metropolis and its activities integrated into a metropolitan system now more than ever before ... The basic form or structure remains; its magnitude is greater and its compaction less. (Wolf 1969 p 142)

Wolf goes on to forecast that:

... The 'hollow metropolis' rather than the 'exploding metropolis' is the characteristic metropolis of contemporary America. Extrapolated to the end of this century, the hollow metropolis of yesteryear will be bigger, more diffused, and more hollow in the future ... If present conditions continue, the hollow metropolis of the future will have a growing inner area which is declining or stagnant in terms of population, where low-income groups, unpopular minority groups, and unemployables of various sorts will predominate. (Wolf 1969 p 153)

The picture is not exactly a cheerful one.

7.3 The urban field Both Gottmann and Wolf have put forward concepts to try and capture the expanding scale of urban life. Freidmann and Miller also felt this need, their aim being to incorporate metropolitan areas and intermetropolitan peripheries into a unified schema. They projected the gradual incorporation of the periphery into the urban realm, the complete entity being termed the 'urban field'. They were anxious not to lay down any rigid or predetermined formulations regarding the physical form of the field, viewing it instead as 'a mosaic of different forms and micro-environments which co-exist within a common communications framework' (Freidmann and Miller 1965 p 317). They see it being far less focused than today's metropolitan areas, whose influence they foresee being attenuated. They summarize their view as follows:

... A new scale of urban living that will extend far beyond existing metropolitan cores and penetrate deeply into the periphery. Relations of dominance and dependency will be transcended. The older established centres, together with the inter-metropolitan peripheries that envelop them, will constitute the new ecological unit of America's post-industrial society that will replace traditional concepts of city and metropolis. This basic element of the emerging spatial order we shall call the 'urban field'. (Freidmann and Miller 1965, p 313, see Reader and Figure 22)

Figure 22 Potential urban fields in the United States   Source: Freidmann and Miller (1965)

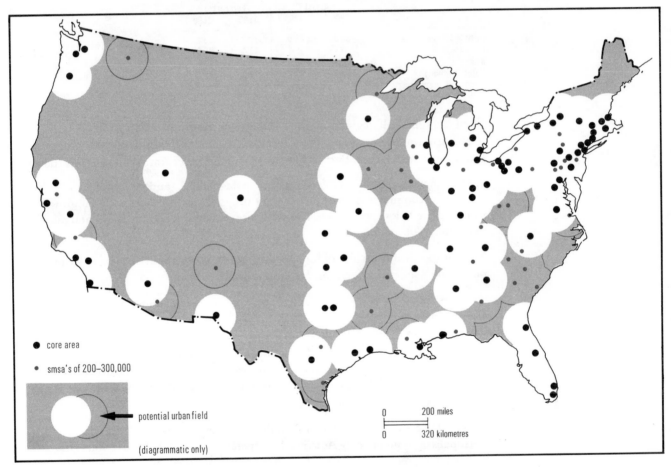

- ● core area
- • smsa's of 200–300,000

→ potential urban field

(diagrammatic only)

0   200 miles
0   320 kilometres

7.4 The non-place urban realm and its critics

We dealt in Unit 30 with some of Melvin Webber's ideas regarding the influence of the diminishing 'friction of space' upon the traditional urban structure, and posed certain criticisms of his transport and communications determinism. Our intention here is not to reiterate this material, but rather to examine Webber's spatial conception of the future and certain opposing views.

The future that Webber envisages is one where the city as traditionally conceived is no longer necessary, and where people and activities, freed from the constraints of space, will diffuse across the land. 'The spatial patterns of American urban settlements are going to be considerably more dispersed, varied, and space-consuming than they ever were in the past . . . disparate spatial dispersion seems to be a built-in feature of the future' (Webber 1963 p 23).

Webber does not envisage the total demise of the traditional city nor a future of homogeneous dispersion. Instead he envisages far more diversified land use pattern, where the land uses themselves are the logical outcome of social processes rather than planning ideologies. He thus rejects the view that: 'urban and rural comprise a dualism that should be clearly expressed in the physical and spatial form of the city, that orderliness depends upon boundedness' (p 34), believing instead that such 'unitary conception of urban places are fast becoming anachronistic'. Critics of such ideas differ, however. Mumford, for instance, has expressed the view that 'a modern city, no less than a medieval town . . . must have a definite size, form, boundary'. So too, Nairn says of the American urban landscape that 'each building is treated in isolation, nothing binds it to the next one: there is a complete failure in relationship' (both quoted in Hall 1968). Webber would answer these critics as follows:

. . . We have often erred, I believe, in taking the visual symbols of urbanization to be marks of the important qualities of urban society; we have compared these symbols with our ideological precepts of order and found they do not conform; and so we have mistaken for 'urban chaos' what is more likely to be a newly emerging order whose signal qualities are complexity and diversity. (Webber 1963 p 25)

Similarly Riley has referred to the 'unspoken assumption that a city is not really a city unless it has two attributes, high density and a centrist orientation' (quoted in Hall 1968).

The question is basically one of opposing value orientations which are unlikely to be resolved. Nevertheless, in so far as Webber's ideas are dependent upon a high level of mass mobility, Sacco's (1972) critique of auto-determinism in Europe is interesting, despite his urbanist orientation. Noting the tendency to refer constantly to the American city as example and pointer, and the systematic, if unconscious utilization of American models when analysing reality, Sacco (1972) states that by extrapolation and projection the United States has become 'the contemporary incarnation of our future' (p 165). Relatively recently, however, American writers themselves have come to realize that the United States is far from homogeneous in terms of urban development, and that major differences in form exist between the older cities of the north and east, and the younger cities of the south and west.

The realization of this differentiation within the USA itself does not weaken Sacco's arguments; on the contrary, it reinforces them, for the differences in the form and culture of western European cities as opposed to American cities is just as great, if not greater, than the differences between American cities themselves. Sacco's argument is basically two-fold and rests on the premises of differences in form and culture. He argues in respect of the former that:

. . . By accepting the hypothesis that private motorization in Europe will follow the same trends as American motorization . . . one fails to consider the 'physical base' on which European civilization is built in relation to the 'physical base' of the United States. (Sacco 1972 p 165)

. . . The evidence cannot escape us that the European city still retains, even in a period of very large and growing wide-spread use of the private car, a density rarely equalled on the other side of the ocean . . .

A dispersed type of habitat, morphologically similar to American middle-class habitats, based on and made possible by generalized use of the private car, is . . . inconceivable around Paris and Rome; for it is basically incompatible with the existence, in the city centres, of spaces and equipment that intensive use of the car requires. (Sacco 1972 p 162)

Sacco is arguing that one cannot say that increasing motorization will necessarily lead to similar city forms, if motorization itself is dependent upon city form to start with, and that these differ. Even if we accept this, and Sacco's further contention that growing motorization *leads* to territorial dispersal rather than the reverse, his argument contains two major weaknesses. The European city may have a higher density than even its eastern American counterpart, but this may be due to historical inertia. Secondly, this may be diminishing, and a time-lag effect may be operating, ie European cities may be dense because they were dense, nevertheless they may be becoming less dense, especially on their peripheries.

Sacco's second major prop is a cultural one. He states that there exists 'a deeply rooted tendency to employ the ground intensively, even where there are no physical limitations, and where historical limitations have passed away' (p 166). He also believes that:

> . . . It would be in vain to look in Europe for the phenomenon of disinterest in the old centre so characteristic of large American metropoles. And it is futile to look for the fragmentation of the urban community into sub-groups that clearly and openly tend to organize themselves into semi-autonomous and territorially separated communities. This is the most important difference between the American *urbanite* and the European *citizen*. (Sacco 1972)

However much we may wish to agree with these cultural statements, it is incumbent upon us to ask whether they reflect more in the way of wishful thinking than hard fact.

7.5 Functional differentiation

Some recent authors like Webber, have come to the conclusion that a concern with form *per se* is an irrelevancy, based on outmoded conceptions of what cities ought to be like, rather than on a concern with social processes and urban functions. John McHale (1970) has gone even further, and believes that the conventional multi-purpose city with its manufacturing, learning, cultural, tourist and other functions is becoming redundant, in the face of increasing mobility, decentralization and technological advance. The multi-functional form, in his view, is largely of the 'implosive compacting' of both people and activities under the accelerating pressures of nineteenth century industrialization, and he sees it as now exhibiting signs of grave instability and obsolescence. As he puts it:

> . . . The 'services' of the city are now available without the need to go within the city walls. For many the city is where one *goes*, variously to the theatre, to shop, to transact business, to talk with a legislator or to have fun.
> The city is tending towards a specialized *service* centre rather than a multi-functional manufacturing, processing and distribution unit. (McHale 1970)

As a result of this, McHale argues that much of our present concern with the designing and planning of ideal city forms is misconceived, we should instead allow for a large number of possible alternatives. He suggests several, namely the ceremonial city, the university city, the scientific city, the festival city, the recreation or fun city, the communications city, the convention conference city, the museum city and the experimental city. Although McHale himself views his typology as a conceptual exercise regarding the future city, two criticisms may be levelled at his underlying idea. First, as he himself frequently admits, this differentiation of function is more incipient than actual. The Las Vegas's and Saratoga Springs of this world are few and far between. They are unique anomalies. Though many cities do have distinct functional leanings they are still by and large multi-functional. Secondly, his picture of the average individual gaily moving from one city to the next is wholly unreal, though it may be true of a small elite of decision makers, artists, jet-set academics and the like, far too much theory is built around this group. Such theorists have been blinded by their own reflected life style.

7.6 The 'inversion' thesis and the 'new rural society'

H. G. Wells, writing in 1902, predicted that:

. . . The city will diffuse itself until it has taken up considerable areas and many of the characteristics of what is not country . . . The country will take itself many qualities of the city. The old antithesis will . . . cease, the boundary lines will altogether disappear . . . To receive the daily paper a few hours late will be the extreme measure of rusticity save in a few remote islands and inaccessible places. (Wells 1902 pp 70–1)

According to Berry:

. . . Achieved at a pace more rapid than he anticipated, Wells' forecasts captured the essential features of the geography of the United States in 1960. 'City' and the continuously built-up 'urbanized area' had already been superseded in the reality of daily life by large urban regions–commuting areas or, as C. A. Doxiades calls them, 'daily urban systems'. (Berry 1970 p 23)

Figure 23 Commuting fields of all major central cities in the United States   Source: Berry (1970)

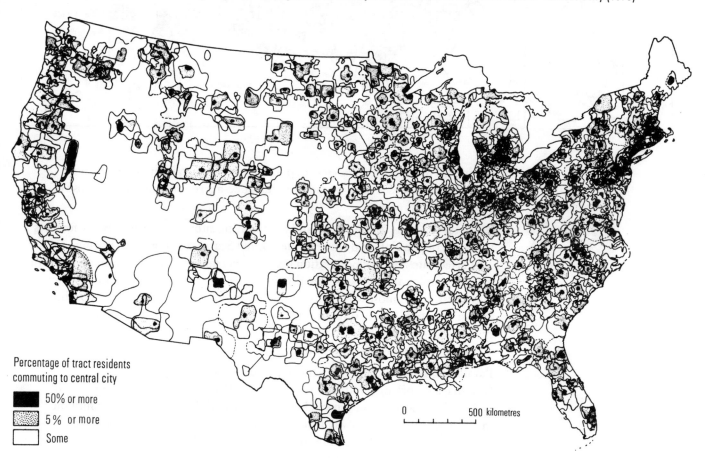

Percentage of tract residents
commuting to central city

■ 50% or more

▨ 5% or more

☐ Some

0   500 kilometres

Berry states that even by 1960, all but five per cent of the population of the USA lived within such daily urban systems (see Figure 23), and terms the zone beyond the *inter-urban periphery*. From these statements of fact, Berry makes a very speculative jump based on the developments in communications technology and some very speculative 'evidence' to the conclusion that: 'We are on the verge of yet another fundamental transformation of American society, one

Figure 24 Zones of population decline in the United States 1950–60 Source: Berry (1970)

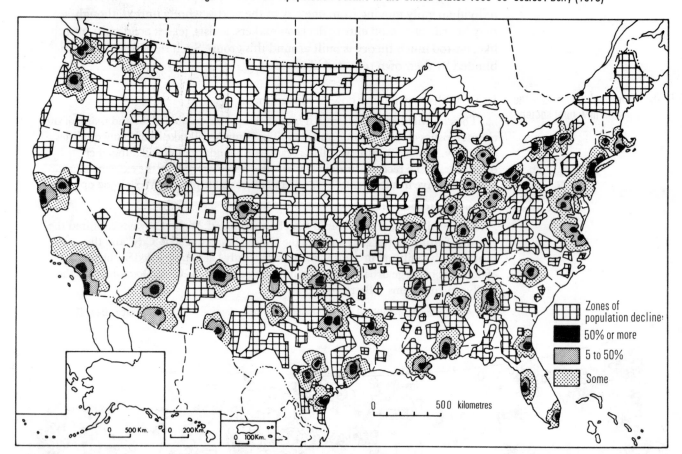

Zones of
population decline:

50% or more

5 to 50%

Some

0   500 kilometres

destined, I anticipate, to *invert* the spatial patterns of 1960 by the year 2000'
(p 43). 'I also foresee that gradients of distance-accretion will replace those of
distance-decay' (p 47).

Thus, on the basis of continued and accelerating suburbanization, Berry foresees
the zones of population decline in the United States (see Figure 24) being
converted into zones of population growth. 'Persons of greater wealth and leisure
will find homes and work among the more remote environments of hills, water
and forest, while most will aspire to this as an ideal' (p 47). Apart from outlining
a possible future for an affluent minority only, Berry's vision is extremely
speculative and goes beyond almost every other conceptualization of the future,
all of which he views as conservative.

Paralleling Berry's ideas, but from a far more normative standpoint, is
Goldmark's work on what he terms the 'New Rural Society'. Arguing that all
of America's population growth between now and the year 2000 (100 million
in all) must be directed away from the cities if these are not to break down
entirely, he believes they should be distributed in existing towns and cities where
the population is 100,000 or less. He calculates that there are well over 5,000
such communities in the United States. New towns are not the answer,
according to Goldmark, as one would have to be built *every third day for the next
thirty years* to handle the increase. Existing population centres on the other
hand are already going concerns more or less well provided with facilities. To
make this possible, however, Goldmark foresees the need for a phenomenal
increase in telecommunications in order to tie them into the commercial,
cultural, educational and recreational activities of the nation. As he puts it:

... These are the things that drew people to the cities in the first place, even though conditions are such that they no longer make use of many of them. Most people want to live in stimulating and attractive environments and we will have to see to it that the rural areas are no longer isolated and deprived of theatres, concerts, opera, museum and sporting events ...

With the present intolerable load removed from the big cities they could revert to what they were supposed to be in the first place as cultural centres and headquarters for business. The best of the urban life and the best of the rural life. That is really what this is all about. And for the first time the technology is available to make it possible. (*The Guardian*, 3 April 1973)

What Goldmark fails to mention is how migration of many of the currently urban poor and deprived could be enabled, without which the New Rural Society would just become white middle class suburbia on a grander scale.

7.7 The hyperurban society

One very general but very useful conception is that of the hyperurban society; its very generality subsuming all the previous concepts at a high level of abstraction. Lionel March (1969 p 4) defines a hyperurban society as one 'in which the distinction between urban and rural has been surpassed. Quite literally it is a society that has transcended the historic and distinct urban and rural ways of life'. March quotes Sorokin and Zimmerman's description of the development of rural-urban differentiation during the history of mankind:

... At the initial stages the differentiation was very slight and insignificant; it continued to grow in subsequent periods of the history of a society or of all mankind; finally having reached its climax, it has begun to be less and less sharp, less and less intensive, and at the present moment in several Western countries it tends to decrease. (Sorokin and Zimmerman 1929)

Figure 25 The development of hyperurban society Source: Swedner (1960)

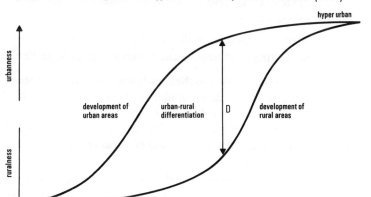

March also refers to Harold Swedner's (1960) illustration of this principle (see Figure 25) such that urban-rural differentiation increases from almost nothing to a maximum and then diminishes again. At present Western societies have passed this maximum point and are heading rapidly towards minimal differentiation once again – a process which all the previous concepts discussed have tried to come to terms with in one way or another.

7.8 Ecumenopolis

The starting point for Doxiades's conception of Ecumenopolis, or world city, is continuing population growth. The population of the Earth is currently some 3,300 million, and most estimates place it at somewhere between

6,500 million and 7,000 million by the end of the century assuming the continuation of present trends. Looking further ahead, Doxiades believes that 'even under the most conservative estimates, and even if effective policies of birth control are implemented, the population of the Earth will be more than 12,000 million a hundred years from now' (Doxiades 1968 p 215), and he sees 20,000–30,000 million as a more realistic figure.

Alongside this, Doxiades points to the levelling off and decline in rural population since the first part of this century. Urban population on the other hand has been increasing rapidly and Doxiades foresees the present ratio of forty-five per cent urban and fifty-five per cent rural, changing to ninety-five per cent and five per cent within one hundred years. In addition Doxiades comments that 'since we have acquired mechanical means of transportation, the ratio of the built-up or settled area to the urban population has been increasing at a much faster rate than the growth of that population' (Doxiades 1968 p 217). This, he believes, will continue for many decades, leading to the inevitable fact that settlements of the future will not be just 7–10 times larger than the present area (ie enlarged by the same coefficient as the population), but maybe 30, 40 or even 50 times as large. If this occurs, says Doxiades, 'it is quite probable that all settlements will become interconnected to form a continuous system covering the inhabitable earth'. It is this that Doxiades terms Ecumenopolis, and according to him we are already witnessing its birth in various parts of the world.

Many strong criticisms can be made of Doxiades's conception. Indeed, Freidmann and Miller state that 'it is no concept at all but a poetic vision'. First, Doxiades's assumptions concerning continued population growth to the levels he envisages are speculative. Secondly, in Britain and many other densely populated areas car ownership is expected to reach saturation point by the end of this century, assuming that is, that a return to more efficient forms of transport does not occur before then, with the associated restraint of increasing physical expansion.

Finally, Doxiades is disturbingly quiescent in his views regarding the possibility of halting or changing the pattern of growth of Ecumenopolis:

... Counteraction to the trends leading to Ecumenopolis is impracticable ... because:
1 these are trends of population growth determined by many biological and social forces which we do not even understand properly, let alone dare countermand.
2 the great forces shaping the Ecumenopolis, such as economic, commercial, social, political, technological and cultural are already being deployed and it is too late to reverse them.

The eventual creation of the Ecumenopolis should therefore be considered an inevitability which we must accept. Our challenge is to make the Ecumenopolis fit for Man. (Doxiades 1968 p 430)

This should be compared with Jenck's criticisms of exactly this type of weak determinism and its dangers:

... Weak determinism asserts that although we can be aware of natural laws and inevitable trends we actually are powerless to *change* them. Thus it tends to undermine our will and reconcile us to that which we *think* is beyond our power ... What effectively happens is that we deny that knowledge of a force allows us to do anything about it. (Jencks 1971)

7.9 The evolving urban form – a personal view

Almost all of the conceptualizations of the evolving urban form we have discussed have some degree of truth, with the possible exception of Doxiades 'Ecumenopolis' which Freidmann and Miller rightly class as more of a poetic vision than a conceptualization. All of them, however, outline a partial picture at most. Whilst agreeing with March that we are moving towards a hyperurban society, this does not help us, except at the most general level, to foresee the likely macro urban future. Gottmann's concept of megalopolis is useful in so far as it describes an alteration in the scale and extent of the urban settlement pattern. It would be a mistake, however, to deduce from this that the city is in the process of disintegrating. As Wolf points out, the integrating role of the metropolitan system is, if anything, greater than ever before. What is happening is that whilst the basic structure remains, 'its magnitude is greater and its compaction less'.

Freidmann and Miller make some move towards the acceptance and analysis of this fact through their concept of the urban field – which is perhaps likely to prove the most accurate partial vision of the future. Combined with the idea of the tidal wave, the urban field certainly appears far more likely than the inversion postulated by Berry which, by his own words, would appear to be confined to an affluent minority. Freidmann and Miller's 'urban field' is not likely to be a reality for the poor and ethnic minorities, but at least it presages a far more socially widespread movement than does Berry's inversion thesis.

The most likely development in the USA and, to a lesser extent, in western Europe would seem to be something of a potpourri. I foresee the development of urban fields in a social, employment and recreational sense, allied with an urban wave of actual residential growth. Allied with this there is likely to be a *partial* inversion along the lines Berry suggests, though nothing as marked as Peter Goldmark's new rural society. One cause of this will be the continued growth of second home ownership (see Unit 23). At the other end of the scale Wolf foresees the development of a growing deprived inner city rump. What should be emphasized is that these are *primary* forecasts *not* secondary ones: that is to say, these trends are not inexorable – they are in part dependent upon social action or the lack of it.

SAQ 18   Attempt to list the eight different conceptualizations of the evolving urban form discussed in Section 7, recalling their main features and any major criticisms.

8 Planning for growth and change

I referred earlier to the danger of attempting to predict 'ideal' forms, for this neglects the processes of change in society and the fact that ultimately form is no more than a temporary convenience – whatever other values we may attach to it. Thomas Paine, deputy head of NASA, put this well when he stated that: 'There are institutions that have become, and institutions that are becoming. Cities are inherently the second. They should never be finished' (quoted in the extract from Davie in the Reader). More specifically, Elher has written:

... We must have built-in rules for adaption, evolution, growth, development, change and obsolescence ... [whereas] ... the traditional urban planner or designer ... has usually conceived ... of the city, in static, artifactual terms. (Elher 1971 p 794)

Our plans, he says, must 'incorporate the intrinsic abilities of the urban system for self-organization' (p 795).

Such statements apart, planning for change is not easy. In fact it is extremely difficult. On the one hand, as Donald Folely has observed, while architects and planners talk of innovation and mobility they ignore the fact that the very permanence of the physical environment they construct promotes inflexibility and stability of pattern. On the other hand, plans cannot be infinitely flexible for then nothing would ever get built. At this juncture the advocates of plug-in or instant architecture and the like would point to their ideas as the real solution. As Albers has pointed out, however, there are several deficiencies in the modular plug-in philosophy. An even more taxing problem would seem to arise regarding the nature of physical planning itself, which White (1969 p 22) defines as 'the translation of social and economic objectives, as derived from the political process, into an efficient spatial arrangement'. The problem stems from Webber's belief that 'spatial separation or propinquity is no longer an accurate indicator of functional relations; and, hence, mere locational pattern is no longer an adequate symbol of order' (Webber 1963 p 49). Webber puts the implications as follows:

... The task of the spatial planner is therefore considerably more difficult than we have traditionally thought. The normative guides that we have used have been orientated primarily to the form aspects that can be represented on maps and have applied static and simplistic concepts of order that are not consonant with the processes of growing and complex urban systems. (Webber 1963 p 49)

Fortunately for physical planning, Webber's conception of affairs is a thing more incipient than actual, based as it is on developments in California. And even if it were wholly a reality this would not entirely remove the logic of physical planning.

SAQ 19   Why is it essential not to plan 'final solutions' for cities, but instead to plan for growth and change?

9 Conclusion   It is quite apparent that the old balance of centripetal and centrifugal forces operating on the city has been profoundly altered. The preference for suburban or exurban living has been able to manifest itself through transportation development, specifically the advent of the private car.

Wolf (1969) sees no prospect of the new balance of forces altering unless there occurs a definite pull towards the centre, based perhaps on some renewed feeling for urbanism. This he views as unlikely, as he does the prospect of a *push* due to the ample land reserves of the United States. The only factor he conceives of as a possible limiting factor is the attitude towards commuting. Wurster, however, sees rising land costs and the rising costs of providing facilities for scattered developments as possible constraints.

Strangely enough, a number of writers including Wolf (1969), Wurster (1963), Grove (1968), and Freidmann and Miller (1965), have all suggested that the growth in second home ownership could at least pave the way, if not lead, to a greater acceptability of compact high density settlements. Grove comments that:

... A two home/long weekend culture would be in a sense a continuation and rationalization of the present tendency for more dispersed living ... We could enjoy – at different times – the *genuinely* urban and *genuinely* rural settings that most people seem to need, and that they seek for vainly in the suburb or low density new town ... The contrast between town and country would be *real* again. (Grove 1968 p 93) (my emphases)

It must be said, however, that this view represents more in the way of wishful thinking than a valid tendency for the future. It is much more likely – unless something is done to try to halt it – that as cities grow in size, so too their suburbs will spread (see Unit 23). 'We may say this in confidence because there is no counter-evidence. In every major modern city for which we have precise statistical data, the frontier of building is being pushed outwards . . . This has been true ever since the development of modern urban transport techniques' (Hall 1966 p 234). The dangers this poses are twofold. Firstly, there is the danger that much of the rural landscape will be overwhelmed, and annexed to the city and its urban field. Secondly, the traditional dimension of the pre-mechanical age – what Le Corbusier termed 'congruent size' – is being increasingly upset as a direct result of the increase in urban size and population. As Ribas i Piera has put it:

. . . The morphological scheme of the old city, with a single centre and limited radius, cannot exist when transposed on a larger dimension – the dimension corresponding to the new city concentrations . . . A city of one million people is not a city of 50,000 inhabitants enlarged like a photograph (Ribas i Piera 1972 p 193)

Such an increase in scale all too frequently results in the values of landscape being no longer accessible in the city, just as the centre is no longer accessible to large parts of the city. The dual problems of scale and form will need to be successfully solved, if we are to live out the next few decades in a satisfactory, if not a pleasing, urban environment.

SAQ 20   What are the dangers posed by continual urban growth?

Answers to SAQs

Answer SAQ 1   The micro urban form consists of specific built forms and their interrelationships. The meso urban form is equivalent to the internal structure of the city. The macro urban form refers to the urban settlement pattern as a whole.

Answer SAQ 2   Urban form is important for different reasons at different scales. At the macro scale the amount of built-up land area and its distribution is important, especially in relation to the amount and distribution of non-urban land. So too, the overall pattern of development clearly has implications for access to the countryside and for its own growth. At the meso level the urban form influences the distribution of homes, workplaces, leisure and recreational facilities, and their accessibility. At the micro level urban form is especially important in the movement patterns engendered, in the stimuli they offer, and in their flexibility.

Answer SAQ 3   Allocational efficiency refers to the total efficiency of a city or a society as a whole in terms of resource maximization. Distributional efficiency refers to the manner in which the resources, products and income of a city or society are distributed.

Answer SAQ 4   Clearly not. The city is not just a functional object whose layout is unimportant, it serves a variety of human psychological needs, some of which are related to physical aesthetics.

Answer SAQ 5   No, neutral criteria are impossible because all criteria are normative in that they set out what should be rather than attempting to describe what is. They are therefore the product of an evaluative selection of what is deemed important.

Answer SAQ 6   1 structural density, 2 the capacity, type and pattern of circulation facilities, 3 the location of large fixed activities, 4 grain, 5 focal organization, and 6 accessibility.

Answer SAQ 7   Only in extreme cases, otherwise density is related to the size and scale of settlements and mediated by technology, culture and affluence.

Answer SAQ 8   Because economic factors more generally function as constraints upon choice rather than as basic dimensions of choice themselves.

Answer SAQ 9   Wurster's classification was formulated on the basis of two variables, a form variable (ranging from extreme concentration to extreme dispersion), and a scale variable (concerned with the level of integration of various activities and functions within the urban complex).

Answer SAQ 10   Point, line and area as expressed in the concentric city, the linear city and the dispersed city.

Answer SAQ 11   Refer to Section 4 for a summary of these.

Answer SAQ 12   The constellation of cities (usually in its 'debased' satellite form), the star and the linear city have been favourably received, both for their better performance on many criteria, and because they require less restructuring of the existing urban fabric than other alternatives. Instead, they all allow development from the basis of the existing form in certain specified directions.

Answer SAQ 13   The principle that the area of each successive band remains equal whilst the width of each band decreases.

Answer SAQ 14   Two and three times as great, respectively.

Answer SAQ 15   March states that, if given the choice, most people would prefer rural living, but that this has usually taken the form of low density ribbon development which is space consuming. He also points out that accessibility to city centres can also be very low in the countryside. He therefore suggests that developments such as one sees around old village greens could, if strung out just off main roads permit rural living, high density and high accessibility.

Answer SAQ 16   They all indicate the concentration of population growth in existing urban regions, the decentralization of population within these regions, and the extension of such regions across ever larger areas.

Answer SAQ 17   Pickard's findings indicated the relative increase of urban population in the 'newer', higher amenity areas of the South and West, which is what the communications theorists have been predicting.

Answer SAQ 18   Refer to Section 7.

Answer SAQ 19   Because society changes and, as it does, so do the built forms of cities which are but functional responses to the changing demands made by man and his changing patterns of organization, production and distribution. Cities should exist for man and not the reverse. In addition, diversity and variety are qualities which stem more from the self-organization of cities than from conscious planning.

Answer SAQ 20   The dangers are twofold. First, and more long term, there is the danger of the increasing annexation of the rural landscape. Secondly, the increasing scale of urban areas is upsetting traditional balances and, as Toynbee points out, potentially trapping man in the city.

References   ALBERS, G. (1968) *Towards a Theory of Urban Structure*, Town and Country Planning Institute Summer School, Manchester.

ALEXANDER, C. (1970) 'Major Changes in Environmental Form required by Social and Psychological Demands' in *Ekistics*, 28, August, pp 78–85.

BELL, G. and TYRWHITT, J. (eds) (1972) *Human Identity in the Urban Environment*, Harmondsworth, Penguin Books.

BERRY, B. J. L. (1970) 'The Geography of the United States in the Year 2000' in *Transactions of the Institute of British Geographers*, 51, pp 21–54.

BOCHERT, J. (1972) 'America's Changing Metropolitan Regions' in *Annals of the Association of American Geographers*, 62, 2, June, pp 352–73.

DELOS THREE SYMPOSIUM (1972) 'Living at High Densities' in BELL and TYRWHITT (1972).

DOXIADES, C. (1968) *Ekistics*, London, Hutchinson.

DOXIADES, C. (1972) 'Anthropocosmos: The World of Man' in BELL and TYRWHITT (1972).

DUBOS, R. (1972) 'The Crisis of Man in his Environment' in BELL and TYRWHITT (1972).

DUHL, L. (1963) 'The Human Measure: Man and Family in Megalopolis' in WINGO, L. (ed) (1963) *Cities and Space*, Baltimore, Johns Hopkins Press.

ELHER, C. (1971) 'Urban Systems Design: Towards an Ecological Rethink' in *American Behavioral Scientist*, 14, 6, pp 781–801.

FREIDMANN, J. and MILLER, J. (1965) 'The Urban Field' in *Journal of the Institute of American Planners*, November, pp 312–20.

GOTTMANN, J. (1957) 'Megalopolis – or the Urbanization of the Northeastern Seaboard' in *Economic Geography*, 33, 3, July, p 189.

GROVE, D. (1968) 'Physical Planning and Social Change' in YOUNG, M. (ed) (1968) *Forecasting and the Social Sciences*, London, Heinemann.

HALL, P. (1966) *The World Cities*, London, World University Library, Weidenfeld and Nicholson.

HALL, P. (1968) 'The Urban Culture and the Suburban Culture' in EELLS, R. and WALTON, C. (eds) (1968) *Man in the City of the Future*, London, Collier-Macmillan.

HARVEY, D. (1971) 'Social Processes, Spatial Form and the Redistribution of Real Income in an Urban System' in Stewart (1972).

JACOBS, J. (1972) *The Death and Life of Great American Cities*, Harmondsworth, Pelican Books.

JENCKS, C. (1971) *Architecture 2000*, London, Studio Vista.

JONES, E. (1971) 'The Future Habitat' in BUCHANAN, R. H. *et al* (eds) (1971) *Man and His Habitat*, London, Routledge & Kegan Paul, pp 247–63.

KELLER, S. (1972) 'Beyond the City: need for a vision' in *American Behavioral Scientist*, 15, pp 591–605.

KIVELL, P. T. (1972) 'A note on Metropolitan areas, 1961–71' in *Area*, 4, 3, pp 179–84.

LYNCH, K. (1961) 'The Pattern of Metropolis' in *Daedalus*, Winter, pp 79–98.

LYNCH, K. and RODWIN, L. (1958) 'A Theory of Urban Form' in *Journal of the American Institute of Planners*, 24, Fall, pp 201–14.

MCHALE, J. (1970) 'Future City(s): Notes on a Typology' in *Ekistics*, 28, pp 86–90.

MARCH, L. (1967) 'Homes Beyond the Fringe' in *RIBA Journal*, August 1967, reprinted in slightly abridged form as 'Let's Build in Lines', *New Society*, 20 July 1967.

MARCH, L. (1969) 'The Spatial Organization of hyper-urban societies', Town and Country Planning Summer School.

MARCH, L. (1972) 'An Examination of Layouts' in *Built Environment*, September, pp 374–8.

MARCH, L. and MARTIN, L. (eds) (1972) *Urban Space and Structures*, London, Cambridge University Press.

PICKARD, J. (1970) 'Is Dispersal the Answer to Urban Overgrowth?' in *Urban Land*, 29, January, pp 3–10.

RAPOPORT, A. and KANTER, D. (1967) 'Complexity and Ambiguity in Environmental Design' in *Journal of the Institute of American Planners*, 33, 4, July, pp 210–21.

RAPOPORT, A. and HAWKES, R. (1970) 'The Perception of Urban Complexity' in *Journal of the Institute of American Planners*, 36, 2, March, pp 106–11.

RIBAS I PIERA, M. (1972) 'The Consumption of Landscape in the City of the Future' in HÄGERSTRAND, T. and VAN HULTEN, M. (eds) (1972) *Europe 2000: Fears and Hopes for a European Urbanization*, The Hague, Martinus Nijhoff.

SACCO, G. (1972) 'Morphology and Culture of European Cities' in HÄGERSTRAND, T. and VAN HULTEN, M. (eds) (1972) *Europe 2000*.

SOROKIN, P. and ZIMMERMAN, C. (1929) *Principles of Rural-Urban Sociology*, London, Holt and Reinhart.

STEWART, M. (ed) (1972) *The City: Problems of Planning*, Harmondsworth, Penguin Books (set book).

SWEDNER, H. (1960) *Ecological Differentiation of Habits and Attitudes*, Lund, Gleerup.

TOYNBEE, A. (1972) 'Has Man's Metropolitan Environment Any Precedents?' in BELL and TYRWHITT (1972).

WEBBER, M. (1963) 'Order in Diversity: Community Without Propinquity' in WINGO, L. (ed) (1963) *Cities and Space*, Baltimore, Johns Hopkins Press.

WELLS, H. G. (1902) *Anticipations of the Reaction of Mechanical and Scientific Progress Upon Human Life and Thought*, London, Chapman and Hall.

WHITE, D. (1971) 'Pressure District' in *New Society*, 465, 26 August 1971, pp 364–6.

WHITE, O. (1969) 'Societal Determinants of Urban form – some thoughts on the city in the year 2000', *Centre for Environmental Studies*, Working Paper 45.

WOLF, L. (1969) 'The Metropolitan Tidal Wave in Ohio, 1900–2000', in *Economic Geography*, 45.

WURSTER, C. B. (1963) 'The Form and Structure of the Future Urban Complex' in WINGO, L. (ed) (1963) *Cities and Space*, Baltimore, Johns Hopkins Press.

Acknowledgements   Grateful acknowledgement is made to the following sources for material used in this unit:

Figure 1: California Department of Transportation; *Figure 2:* New Society for David White, 'Pressure District' in *New Society*, 26 August 1961; *Figure 3:* The Johns Hopkins University Press for C. B. Wurster, 'The form and structure of the future urban complex' in *Cities and Space* (ed L. Wingo); *Figures 4 and 18a, b, c:* Town and Country Planning Summer School and the authors for G. Albers, 'Towards a theory of urban structure' (1968) and L. March 'The spatial organization of hyperurban societies' (1969); *Figures 5 and 6:* Cambridge University Press for Martin and March, *Urban Space and Structure; Figures 8 and 10:* Built Environment and the author for L. March, 'An examination of layouts' in *Built Environment*, September 1972; *Figure 13:* Allen Lane for Mary Banham in Reyner Banham, *Los Angeles: The Architecture of Four Ecologies*, Allen Lane The Penguin Press 1971 © Reyner Banham 1971; *Figure 14:* Pergamon Press Limited for J. H. Johnson, *Urban Geography: An Introductory Analysis* (1972); *Figure 15:* ULI – The Urban Land Institute, 1200 18th Street, NW, Washington, DC 20036 for J. Pickard, 'Is dispersal the answer to urban overgrowth?' Copyright 1970 reprinted with permission; *Figures 16, 17, 23 and 24:* Institute of British Geographers for P. T. Kivell, 'A note on metropolitan areas, 1961–1971' in *Area*, 4, 3, 1972 and B. Berry 'Geography of the US in the year 2000' in *Transactions of the Institute of British Geographers*, 51, November 1970; *Figure 20 and Table 1:* Clark University for J. Gottmann 'Megalopolis' in *Economic Geography*, 33, 1957 and L. G. Wolf, 'The metropolitan tidal wave in Ohio, 1900–2000' in *Economic Geography*, 45, 1969; *Figure 22:* The American Institute of Planners for J. Freidmann and J. Miller, 'The urban field' in Journal of the Institute of American Planners, 31, 1965. Reproduced by permission; *Figure 25:* C. W. K. Gleerup for H. Swedner, *Ecological Differentiation of Habits and Attitudes*.

Unit 32 Goals for urban development
Philip Sarre

Part cover : Palma Nova (Aerofilms)

Goals for urban development

Aims
The aims of this unit are:
1 To emphasize that the nature of the future city and society are to a considerable degree open.
2 To suggest that short-term policies should be directed toward a stated set of long-term goals.
3 To explore the kinds of goals which may be appropriate for urban development.
4 To indicate procedures which will allow a democratic goal-directed planning.

Objectives
After reading this unit you should be able to:
1 Recognize the main goals implicit in a number of typical pieces of utopian literature.
2 Recognize the main goals of the planning profession in a number of time periods.
3 Criticize the planning process as it operates in this country especially on the grounds of political legitimacy and lack of variety.
4 Sketch in the outlines of a future planning process which suffers less from these inadequacies.

Reading guide
The following is *required reading* and will be assessed in the examination:
1 The correspondence text, 'Goals for urban development'.
2 The Reader excerpt by Banham, R. *et al* in association with Section 4 of the unit. The Ecologist excerpt from *A Blueprint for Survival*, recommended with this unit, is required reading for Unit 33.
3 The Reader article by Webber, in association with Section 4.1 of the unit. The section on pages 282–4, explaining why government intervention is needed, would be an appropriate entry to this unit for anyone who is unwilling to accept the assumption that the future must be planned.
4 The Reader article by Alexander, in association with Section 4.2 of the unit.
A number of Reader extracts are highly relevant to the argument and will aid your understanding, although they will not be directly assessed. We recommend you to read them if you can spare the time.
More, 'Utopia', parallels Section 2.1.
Huxley, 'Brave New World' (Section 2.5)
Meyerson, 'Utopian traditions and the planning of cities' (Sections 2 and 2.5)
Howard, 'Social cities' (Section 3.2)
Le Corbusier, 'A contemporary city' and
Wright, 'City of the future. . . .' (Section 3.3)
Milton Keynes Development Corporation, 'The nature of the plan' (Section 3.4)
Davidoff, 'Normative Planning' (Section 4.1)
Mumford, 'Retrospect and Prospect' (Section 5)

Self-assessment questions and comments
We strongly encourage you to attempt the self-assessment questions – they take a goal-oriented perspective more consistently than is possible in the correspondence text. To encourage you to do this, or at least read the comments on SAQs, some new material has been included in most comments. They are not only a rehash of earlier material.

1 Introduction

This block takes the view that future urban development should be planned. Planning must accommodate to reality, so Units 30 and 31 have described some trends and constraints. This unit concentrates on the goals that future planning might pursue. Although setting goals is inherently idealistic, it is not the intention to lay down a totally unattainable set of goals: by concentrating on goals which are practicable in the foreseeable future one may escape the charge of Utopianism. Nor is the derivation of a final set of goals envisaged: goal-setting should be the prerogative of society at large not an individual or small group within society. Also, since the compatibility among sets of goals will vary with local circumstances, the optimum set of goals can only be determined for specific cases. Lastly, we may be confident that the inhabitants of the twenty-first century will have rather different aspirations from those of today.

Although this course is concerned with urban development, we cannot consider goals only at the level of the city. Cities are subsystems of a larger society and are very much influenced by that society even where they are large enough to influence it significantly in turn. It is thus necessary to look at goals for society at large, whether at a national or world scale. Cities are made up of large numbers of subsystems – groups, institutions and individuals – and goals at this level are also essential. It may often occur that goals at different levels are in conflict. For example, if all the residents of a city were to achieve their goal of car ownership, the urban goal of easy movement would become impossible. Or, the social goal of the most efficient use of capital investment might involve enforcement of shift working which would hamper individuals' social life. The existence of these conflicting goals is one of the major problems of the politician and the planner. In a democracy, it would appear to be the presumption that the overall goal is to maximize satisfaction at the individual level, although it is impossible to satisfy everyone all of the time. In practice, however, it seems to be true that the spontaneous forces in society give very large satisfaction to a small minority, modest satisfaction to the majority and hardly any to another minority. The function of politician and planner is to regulate the distribution of goal satisfaction at the individual level by the use of the most efficient technical and fiscal means at urban and societal levels.

The first half of this unit will explore a range of goals which have been thought relevant in the past, and which seem likely to remain so in the future. Two sources will be used: the tradition of Utopian literature and the theory and practice of city planning. The former illustrates the sorts of goals which have seemed worth pursuing to authors limited only by their imagination, the latter those which have been actively tackled by planners operating under very severe constraints. The former emphasizes arrangements at societal level, the latter at the urban level, though the ultimate goals of both have often been at an individual level. The second half of the unit (including several required readings) will sketch in a future planning process which may be appropriate to the sorts of goals which seem most likely in the foreseeable future.

2 Utopian goals

In a block which deals with the future, it may seem odd to find reference to a literary *genre* which has existed continuously for hundreds of years and has examples dating back thousands. In fact this is not so: the goals which are relevant to future societies relate to some fundamental human questions which have attracted the attention of thinkers from the earliest times. The technological means have changed and economic resources have grown, but the problem of goals remains. Perhaps our greatest advantage is that we can profit from the ideas and mistakes of past thinkers; to attempt to prescribe for the future without reference to the past would squander this advantage.

Rapid study of a wide and complex *genre* from a particular point of view is not uncommon in academic life, but raises serious problems in the Open University system. Ideally we would like you to read original works and make your own assessment of their goals. Time prevents this within the confines of the present course, though we hope some of you will be moved to read on in future. At the opposite extreme, we could present lists of the goals involved in various works. This would have two disadvantages. First, it would dissect the complex wholes of utopian models to reveal only one aspect. This would lose one of the great virtues of utopian writing – the communication of the 'feel' of a society as a human environment and demonstration of the complex interaction between facets of the society. The second disadvantage is that it would reduce your participation. To avoid these problems we have adopted a compromise approach. The unit will provide brief descriptions of the work, with emphasis on goals but also including other relevant material. At the end of each section self-assessment questions will invite you to consider the major goals of the work and our answers will give you a check.

The number of utopian recipes is such that this unit can do no more than provide a selective *hors d'oeuvres*. Rather than surveying a wide range of work for its own sake it will look at four well known utopias and draw out a range of goals which are of general importance.

2.1 More's utopia

The island Kingdom of Utopia, which gave its name to the whole *genre*, was presented by Thomas More as a real place discovered by a voyager, Raphael Hythloday. In fact its existence as a real place is rendered dubious by the fact that the dimensions given by More cannot be mapped (Goodey 1970) but this is, of course, irrelevant to More's purpose. The sources of this ideal state appear

Figure 1 A woodcut of More's Utopia from the Basle edition of 1518
(The Master and Fellows of Trinity College, Cambridge)

to be England and Europe in More's time with elements of classical Rome and Greece. For example, there are fifty-four counties, as in England at that time, but they are organized like Greek city states with towns planned, in Roman fashion, in a rectangular shape.

The social system of Utopia was an idealization, indeed almost a reversal, of those current in More's time. Perhaps the greatest single difference lies in the absence of private property and of income differentials. This is intended to remove exploitation by the rich and dishonesty in the poor. It succeeds, with the addition of social surveillance and sanctions, in eliminating almost all forms of vice. Authority is wielded by a hierarchy of elected officials, from Philarch or Syphogrant (in charge of forty families) through Tranibore to prince. Overcentralization of authority is avoided by a strict law that political matters can only be discussed in public: officials thus cannot plot for their own ends. The function of the Syphogrants 'is to see and take heed that no man sit idle', but also that he is 'not to be wearied with continual work' (More 1910 p 64). In fact almost the whole population is required to do nine hours work a day in farming or the crafts. There is also a regular rotation from country to town and vice versa to ensure that all are competent farmers. Rural produce is exchanged for urban artifacts, though apparently according to no fixed scheme of accounting. The island council, composed of Tranibores and presided over by the prince, balances the surpluses and deficits of the county towns. The surplus over the whole island is exported to neighbouring countries where one-seventh is given to the poor and the remainder sold, often on credit, to increase the wealth of Utopia. Utopia's system of production and exchange, free from idleness and intended only to produce a Spartan material standard of living, is extremely successful and a trade surplus is guaranteed because they import only iron, gold and silver.

The country is perhaps more easily faulted as a place to live, chiefly because of its strict surveillance of people's activities. The work, although unavoidable, is not unduly lengthy even by modern standards, but choice of activity in the seven hours of leisure is constrained: meals are taken in a communal dining hall under the watchful eye of the Syphogrant and free time is expected to be devoted to some wholesome activity such as listening to a lecture or to music. Natural pleasures are approved of, including such diverse activities as 'contemplation of truth', 'meat and drink', 'natural easement', 'the act of generation' or 'scratching' (More 1910 p 90) – but only to a degree consistent with proper health. The general assumption behind More's tone is that almost all Utopians concur with this set of values and that they find their leisure both agreeable and valuable. However, opportunity to dissent is limited – there are 'neither wine tavern, nor ale-house, nor stews, nor any occasion of vice and wickedness' – and the Syphogrant is alert. For most offences there is no set punishment but for those leaving their own county twice without permission and for adulterers the punishment is slavery for an indefinite period. These punishments may not have been severe in More's day, especially when balanced by the undoubted welfare benefits of a place to live and necessary food, clothes, medical care and other materials, but they do suggest a willingness to repress unauthorized desires. This contrasts with the attitude to religion where complete freedom is allowed, in the expectation that almost all will choose to follow the worship of Mithra – the one true religion.

A considerable degree of ambivalence also characterizes the Utopian attitude to war. War is not regarded as a source of glory or heroism – but it is prosecuted with energy and success. The sole use of Utopia's economic surplus is to finance foreign wars – either on behalf of some Utopian merchant, to liberate a country from tyranny or on behalf of some friendly country (though they avoid treaty obligations). Utopian citizens are committed to battle as a last resort; they prefer to sap the enemy's morale by offering a price for the capture or killing of their leaders and to hire foreign mercenaries to do the fighting. The latter allows them to hire the most savage soldiers available, giving them the double reward of success in battle and of reducing the numbers of savage and aggressive people in foreign countries. Military success is turned to economic profit by making defeated enemies pay for the war. Even though Utopians are rarely used in battle they are not allowed to grow decadent: all Utopians, both male and female, perform regular military exercise. Abroad, then, there is no doubt that might is identified with right.

Overall, there is no doubt that Utopia is highly successful in material terms. This is achieved mainly by restricting wants rather than by increasing productive efficiency: the only technological advance employed in Utopia is an artificial incubator for hatching chicks. It also is free from many of the worst features of sixteenth century England. However, material security and social equality are achieved at the price of requiring a dull conformity. This should not be overemphasized because every society exerts some social pressure on its inhabitants to conform to the prevailing norms. The odd thing about Utopia is that, although the political process is open and there is no hereditary power elite, the nature of the society seems hardly to have changed since its founding by King Utopus 1,700 years previously. This introduces two features common to many pieces of utopian work – the tendency to invent ideal people to inhabit the ideal society and to assume that the ideal society will cease to develop. While it may be logically impossible to construct an ideal society to contain far from ideal people, it seems to be unduly pessimistic to assume that the inhabitants of Utopia can only be prevented from spoiling it by prohibiting all change. Surely the combined wisdom of the citizens of Utopia would be better qualified to perfect their society than is any author in a real society.

SAQ 1   What seems to have been More's chief goal at the individual level?

SAQ 2   What appear to have been the goals of Utopia at the societal level?

SAQ 3   In what ways do you think Utopia falls short of being an ideal society?

2.2 Erewhon   The theme of development was taken up by Samuel Butler two and a half centuries later. Butler used the same approach as More – the report of a journey to a previously unknown land. In commenting on the education system of Erewhon, Butler emphasizes that it seems better designed to check mental development than foster it. This is achieved by constant study of the language of hypothetics which is quite useless in real life (the parallel with Latin is obvious). The nature of education and its link to progress is indicated by the fact that Butler's one consolation for the foolishness of the Erewhonian colleges is that 'Were it not for a certain priggishness which these places infuse into so great a number of their alumni, genuine work would become dangerously common' (Butler 1970 p 192). In fact, though the Erewhonians are suspicious of progress, this is only because it is liable to 'lead to self-seeking and unamiability'. If a man can carry his neighbours with him there are no objections.

It is necessary to include a caution before setting out any details of the goals of Erewhonian society. Butler's obvious intent was to parody Victorian England

but his enthusiasm is such that he frequently parodies his parody. He shows a stunning ability to debunk any social arrangement and while this is a useful balance for the rather dogmatic certainties of More, it does lead to difficulties of interpretation. It would not be fair to berate Butler for the inconsistencies in his exposition, however, for they are deliberate:

... this merciful provision of nature, this buffer against collisions, this friction which upsets our calculations but without which existence would be intolerable, this crowning glory of human invention whereby we can be blind and see at one and the same moment, this blessed inconsistency, exists here as elsewhere (Butler 1970 p 131).

The chief inconsistency in the nature of the Erewhonians is that while they are handsome and of pleasing manner, they live in beautiful houses and eat delicious food, they are amiable and uncompetitive, they are also inhuman and hypocritical. The contrast is most starkly shown in their treatment of those who steal and those who are ill. Stealing is treated with the utmost sympathy. True, treatment by the 'straightener' may be highly uncomfortable, but there is no disgrace in the eyes of society. Illness, on the contrary, is a criminal offence and is punished by imprisonment with hard labour. Indeed, so severe is the punishment that it often causes further illness and this is punished even more severely – leading often to a swift death. In contrast to the Victorian system of criminal law, the Erewhonian treatment of illness is highly successful: illness is very rare.

A double paradox occurs in the area of Erewhonian religion. The institutions most like English churches are the Musical Banks. These occupy large ornate buildings with stained glass windows and choirs. However, they have no spiritual function whatever. They issue a coinage which is said by all to be far superior to that issued by commercial banks, but which is of no use at all since commerce, even tipping the staff of the Musical Banks, is conducted in the other currency – which is universally declared to be worthless. The only function of this duplicity seems to be to parody Victorian attitudes to church and bank.

However, a further duplicity exists in the area of worship: the Erewhonians profess to worship personal gods of justice, strength, hope, fear, love, etc. and have an extensive mythology. However, Higgs, the English traveller, discerns that 'their only religion was that of self-respect and consideration for other people' (Butler 1970 p 159). The highest exponents of this humanistic 'religion' were very close to Butler's image of the English gentleman. Typically, although this is the Erewhonian's main religion, it is devoid of formalism and is denied by all.

The most remarkable aspect of Erewhonian society from a modern perspective is the prohibition of machines. On this subject Butler's facetiousness is muted for it relates to evolution, a subject which fascinated him. Some 500 years before Higgs' visit, Erewhon had developed technically rather beyond the stage reached by England in 1870. However an Erewhonian scholar had published a book which demonstrated that, just as the evolution of animals had overtaken that of plants, so the evolution of machines was overtaking that of man. Machines were already more powerful and more exact in physical labour. Machines were available to calculate more rapidly and accurately than man. Their progress was so rapid that the author anticipated the possibility of their developing the ability to communicate, achieving consciousness and the ability to reproduce themselves. His thesis was so powerful that a majority of the people joined the anti-machinist party and, after a civil war which halved the population, all machines developed in the preceding 271 years were destroyed.

The question of the role of the machine has long troubled utopian authors and, with the development of computers, Butler's worries about consciousness and autonomy have become more widespread. However, since the material benefits of machine production and transport are so great, few utopias have dispensed with machines altogether. Dystopias, on the other hand, have tended to emphasize the negative role of advanced technology. In spite of this, conventional expectations of the future include more and better machines. The relation of technology and society is one of the main problems of future design and will remain so. The societies devised by Bellamy and Morris resolve the problem in different ways without going to the extremes occupied by Butler or the dystopians.

SAQ 4 What are Erewhon's chief goals at the individual level?

SAQ 5 What goals exist at higher levels?

2.3 Looking backward 2000–1887

Edward Bellamy's Utopia was experienced by a citizen of nineteenth century Boston who was awoken from a mesmeric trance in the year 2000. There is no attempt to provide an account of how his story came to be published in 1888.

As befits a Utopia set in the future, there is an attempt, though brief, to provide a description of how the millennium was achieved. This is presented as a natural extension of nineteenth century trends. The trend towards concentration of capital led towards plutocracy but contained its own negation for it led on to concentration of all capital in the state, in Bellamy's words:

> ... The nation, that is to say, organized as the one great business corporation in which all other corporations were absorbed; it became the one capitalist in the place of all other capitalists, the sole employer, the final monopoly in which all previous and lesser monopolies were swallowed up, a monopoly in the profits and economies of which all citizens shared. (Bellamy 1890 p 56)

Bellamy's state socialist system is often criticized because labour is compulsory

and the state the only employer. This is said to be totalitarian in the worst sense. However, in any society it is necessary that a certain amount of work be done and in an egalitarian society it seems entirely fair that everyone should do an equal amount of work. Since the education system is open to all and work is allocated on the basis of aptitude and choice, the hardship seems small. Equality of labour is assured because the hours of work are varied to offset the varying pleasantness of different tasks. Finally, it must be appreciated that labour is not viewed as an end in itself but as a means of producing and distributing material abundance. The efficiency of the system used in 2000, gained by reducing wasteful competition and 'gambling' as well as technological advances like pneumatic tubes for transporting goods, mean that each citizen need only work between the ages of 21 and 45. For those who consider this excessive, it is possible to retire at 33 on half the normal income.

... A credit corresponding to his share of the annual product of the nation is given to every citizen on the public books at the beginning of each year, and a credit card issued him with which he procures at the public storehouses, found in every community, whatever he desires whenever he desires it. (Bellamy 1890 p 87)

This credit is equal for every man, woman and child. It says much for the size of the credit and the lack of appetite for goods that people rarely spend their whole income but surrender their surplus to the state. The surplus is spent on 'public works and pleasures in which we all share, upon public halls and buildings, art galleries, bridges, statuary, means of transit and the conveniences of our cities, great musical and theatrical exhibitions, and in providing on a vast scale for the recreations of the people'. These recreations, which may be said to be the goals towards which the society looks, range from the higher exercise of the faculties to sports and games. They are all freely chosen since 'there is far less interference of any sort with personal liberty nowadays than you were accustomed to' (Bellamy 1890 p 116).

Although Congress still exists as a political forum through which change can be sought there appears to be no public pressure for it and if it did exist it would clearly be treated with great caution by those in authority. Conservatism is guaranteed because promotion within the industrial army is gained at first from above, while at more senior levels and in political offices, such as President, elections are held in which only the retired are qualified to vote. Division between leisured class and disenfranchised workers is made on the basis of age.

SAQ 6 What did Edward Bellamy state to be the goals at the individual level of the United States in the year 2000?

SAQ 7 How are these goals reflected at the urban level?

SAQ 8 What are the goals of the society?

2.4 News from nowhere

William Morris published *News from Nowhere* in 1891, four years after *Looking Backward*. The form is strikingly similar – a Victorian Englishman finds himself in the England of the early years of the third millennium. Morris' Utopia is also socialist, but is very different in atmosphere. His account of the revolutionary period notes that state socialism was partly adopted – but only succeeded in upsetting the capitalists without providing a sensible alternative. It did encourage worker unrest which led through strikes and demonstrations to a civil war after which anarchist socialism prevailed.

In Nowhere there are no laws, no private property and no nation states. In

Figure 3 Title page of Kelmscott Press edition of News from Nowhere 1892
(University of London Library)

NEWS FROM NOWHERE: OR, AN EPOCH OF REST, BEING SOME CHAPTERS FROM A UTOPIAN RO, MANCE, BY WILLIAM MORRIS.

Figure 4 Frontispiece of the same (University of London Library)

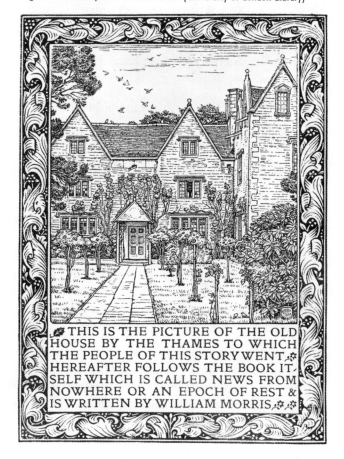

THIS IS THE PICTURE OF THE OLD HOUSE BY THE THAMES TO WHICH THE PEOPLE OF THIS STORY WENT. HEREAFTER FOLLOWS THE BOOK IT. SELF WHICH IS CALLED NEWS FROM NOWHERE OR AN EPOCH OF REST & IS WRITTEN BY WILLIAM MORRIS.

personal matters complete freedom exists and in community matters decisions are taken by a majority of the Mote of the area, called variously the commune, ward or parish. However, the freedom is not chaos – people know what is needed and have a desire to work. Also the task is less severe because society is no longer burdened with the production of sham necessities. Production is geared to known need and the relationship to machines is simple in the extreme. 'All work which would be irksome to do by hand is done by immensely improved machinery; and in all work which it is a pleasure to do by hand machinery is done without' (Morris 1891 p 108).

The craft ethic is extremely powerful. We are told that there was a period after the Revolution when it looked as if society would settle for 'a dull level of utilitarian comfort' (Morris 1891 p 149) but that the remedy was found in art. This both gives individuals satisfaction and guards against the danger of over production. The satisfactions of artistic workmanship are complemented by those of a cheerful community life, and, for rarer souls, by the study of science.

The society does not have goals in any long-term sense but in the immediate sense of getting the best out of the simple things of everyday life. Perhaps it is only the construction of beautiful buildings which lengthens the time scale, but even these tend to be domestic.

The main problem of Morris' scheme is not concerned with the kind of human environment it provides but with its practicability. Can a modern society, even one of modest material use, continue to function without any administration? True, there are few systems which operate over a larger spatial scale than that of the commune, but we are given no indication of how they are organized. Such things as rivers and roads must be managed and raw materials imported from abroad and one would expect systems of coordination and credit – but these are expressly ruled out. Morris provides many persuasive arguments to support his case that humanity will rise to the occasion given the surroundings he describes. No one can prove him wrong, but we should preserve a healthy scepticism.

SAQ 9   What were Morris' goals at the individual level?

SAQ 10   What higher levels of organization contribute to these goals?

2.5 Dystopia and eupsychia

We will not look in detail at any particular dystopia but will survey some common themes. Aldous Huxley's *Brave New World* and George Orwell's *1984* are the best known dystopian novels but many others show similar features. Two aspects of dystopian societies are outstanding: first, political power is highly concentrated and, second, technology is advanced sufficiently to give the authorities powers of surveillance, influence and coercion. Although the material standard of living may be adequate, or even generous, social and spiritual life is crippled. The depth of awareness of self and others is illustrated by the passage from *Brave New World* in the Reader and we recommend you to read this, or preferably the whole book.

Although there are those who might argue that individual awareness and development are not necessarily the highest criteria by which one should judge a society, it is hard to contemplate with equanimity a society in which most people are reduced to the status of robots. The Reader extract from *The Machine Stops* by E. M. Forster shows that, even when people are maintained in complete material comfort, lack of contact with other people and with nature can lead to absolute futility.

Although Meyerson (1961) pronounces the utopian tradition to be dead, except in so far as it has been incorporated into the planning process, Manuel (1965) maintains that the focus has shifted away from the production of social systems and towards an assessment of psychological needs and capacity. A preliminary task of these recent authors was to refute the pessimistic heritage of Darwin and Freud. Darwin's evolutionary ideas had been extended by some thinkers into the doctrine of social Darwinism – which suggested that only a society based on competition could be expected to evolve satisfactorily. Freud's ideas about frustration, repression and aggression made it appear extremely unlikely that human beings could be induced to behave in a civilized way, let alone develop into ideal citizens of an ideal state.

Ideas about evolution were developed in a more optimistic direction by Teilhard de Chardin (1959), Julian Huxley (1960) and their followers. They maintain that man is in the process of, or on the point of, evolving into a higher state of consciousness. This new process of psychosocial evolution will leave man humane, cooperative and rational – and thus ideally suited to inhabit utopia. However, until such time as their prophecy comes about it is impossible to do more than judge its plausibility; it can be neither proved nor disproved.

The opponents of Freud were able to build on ideas which originated in the socialist utopia of Fourier (1849). Wilhelm Reich was the first to put the case that aggression could be prevented by avoiding repression. Reich's case was developed by Erich Fromm, Herbert Marcuse, Norman Brown and Abraham Maslow. The core of their argument is that if every individual is allowed to develop his own potential without excessive cultural repression non-aggressive and altruistic behaviour will predominate. Again, their arguments suggest that it may be possible to develop ideal men to inhabit utopia, but their contentions are yet to be proved.

2.6 Summary

This brief survey of utopian literature has brought a range of goals to our attention. At the individual level, they all provide all citizens with an adequate material standard of living. This feature is also found in dystopias but there the equality which characterizes utopias is notable by its absence. In the most appealing utopias individuals have free choice of recreational activities and, in some, of work as well. This choice is absent in dystopia.

Little emphasis is laid on the urban arrangement of utopia, though it seems frequently very beautiful and orderly. A strong impression is given that urban planning is not needed in an ideal society. Similarly the goals of the society seem usually to be to encourage individuals to achieve satisfaction rather than to urge the society to achieve some aggregate outcome of the growth, empire-building or communism-resisting type so frequent in reality. Even in More's Utopia, where external relations play a major part, charity is a main item of policy.

In addition to suggesting this range of goals, the literary utopias bring four main themes to our attention. First, the tension between the goals of efficient provision of material needs and humane development of individual awareness. Second, the nearly static nature of many utopias, even when they are located in the future. Third, the role of technology – often a major feature of dystopia, but capable, as in *News from Nowhere*, of entirely freeing us from unpleasant work. Fourth, the perfection of man – simultaneously a goal and a prerequisite of achieving utopia.

The range of plausible futures presented by utopian authors ranges very nearly from heaven to hell. The main problem they leave us with is that they give virtually no guidance as to how we may attain the future of our choice. To rectify this imbalance, we will now look at planning – where the constraints are so strong as to divert almost all attention away from goals.

3 Planning goals

Our survey of utopia has suggested a range of goals which have seemed worthwhile to intending architects of the ideal society. The cynic may, however, reject these goals as unrealistic. Hence, we shall now examine the sort of goals which have been pursued by the eminently realistic profession of town planning. What follows is not a brief history of planning since in its concentration on goals it neglects the changes in the techniques used by the profession. As well as suggesting what goals are currently practicable, the review of planning ideas has a second important function since future planning must develop in some way from the present profession. Knowledge of the development of planning in the past may give some indication of the way it

Figure 5 Back to back housing, Leeds (Aerofilms)

will develop in the future. Although towns were planned, in whole or in part, at much earlier times, city planning as a self-conscious movement and profession emerged in the second half of the nineteenth century. It was stimulated by the growth of large industrial cities and was, and still is, essentially concerned to mitigate the evils which resulted from the free play of market forces. These have been extensively described in Part 1 of Ashworth's book *The Genesis of British Town Planning* (1954).

As was the case with literary utopias, this unit can no more than scratch the surface of the history of planning. Fortunately, it is not necessary to do more: the major goals of planners as people and planning as a process can be revealed by a small number of sketches of activity in different periods of time. The focus will be on England, although Europe and the USA also play a strong part.

3.1 Mid-nineteenth century

Perhaps the most striking town planning scheme under way in the mid-nineteenth century was the regularization of Paris under Baron Haussmann. This scheme was remarkable both for its results and in terms of the approach used. The planning phase was preceded by a year-long survey of the city's layout and history. Maps and a historical account were produced. The plan had two main goals and two lesser ones. Perhaps the dominant goal was to enhance the *circulation* of traffic and thus link the many almost self-contained communities into one great city. After this came *ventilation* – creating open spaces to allow fresh air to penetrate into the dense mass of buildings. The two secondary goals were also associated with the new system of broad straight routes primarily intended for circulation: these allowed the army and police to deal much more effectively with rioters than they could in the existing warren of alleyways and provided scope for new aesthetic features. These are classed as secondary goals because they seemed so to Haussmann (Choay 1972 pp 18–19), although they have been emphasized by some of his detractors. The scale of Haussmann's 'surgery' is indicated by the fact that 27,000 of the 66,500 houses in Paris were demolished to make way for roads and open spaces.

Haussmann's bold scheme was emulated, though not with equal thoroughness, in many cities, mostly in Europe but also in the United States. In London a slightly different way of achieving the goal of easy circulation was found. Although Joseph Paxton put forward a proposal to link London's main railway stations by a multi-level railway and road route, the major transport innovation

Figure 6 Map of the Circle Line with dates of some stations (London Transport Executive)

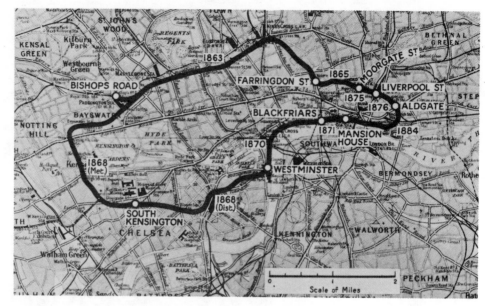

was the Underground railway. The first lines, the Metropolitan Railway (1863) and Inner Circle (1884) were in shallow tunnels but deep tubes were employed from the 1890s. London's transport was thus assured without the massive destruction seen in Paris.

This meant that 'ventilation', reduction in density, did not occur in Britain as a result of road improvements. However, efforts to remove the worst health hazards were already in train. A sanitary movement had been growing during the first half of the century, led by Edwin Chadwick, and, after an epidemic of cholera had shown that disease could easily spread from chronically insanitary slums to the houses of the prosperous, the first Public Health Act was passed in 1848. Local authorities were given powers to install sewers and a pure water supply and to clean streets. A parallel movement was concerned to improve the quality of working class housing. From the 1840s various associations and trusts, such as the Metropolitan Association for Improving the Dwellings of the Industrious Classes and the Peabody Trust, began providing accommodation, often in tenements. Their efforts were, however, very limited in comparison with the rapid increase of population and speculative housing.

Figure 7 Peabody Square, Islington: a near contemporary print (Peabody Trust)

The 1850s also saw the beginning of a project which markedly accelerated an established trend: the building of model villages. This tradition, which began with Samuel Oldnows' Marple, and Robert Owen's New Lanark at the end of the eighteenth century, added the goals of social and moral regeneration and contact with the countryside to the sanitary reform practised in urban settings. The new impetus was given by Titus Salt, a Bradford industrialist, who built a new woollen factory in a country area outside the city and a model village to house his employees. Moderate density, generous facilities and precautions against air and water pollution provided an environment free from many of the worst features of Victorian cities – and even yielded a small profit to Salt. Workers' villages are open to a range of interpretations: at one extreme they may be seen as the homage of employers to the principles of social justice, a more sceptical commentator might balance the real environmental benefits against the odious paternalism of the arrangement and, at the other extreme, they may be seen as a way of eroding the workers' bargaining position in industrial disputes. Whatever the motivation, no increase in scale over that of Saltaire occurred until the building of Port Sunlight from 1888 and Bournville from 1893.

Thus, in the middle of the nineteenth century planning was beginning to emerge as a necessary function of central and local government. Two main goals were apparent: the improvement of public health and urban transport. A third goal occupies a lesser position: the preservation of public order. The fourth goal, of improving working class housing, was pursued by philanthropists. Aesthetic considerations, the main goal of earlier planning, were of minor importance.

SAQ 11   In what ways were the goals of mid-nineteenth century planners and reformers similar to and in what ways different from those of the utopian tradition?

3.2 The turn of the century

By the turn of the century, aesthetic aspects of town planning had made a strong comeback. This was mainly due to a book published by an Austrian, Camillo Sitte, in 1889. Sitte analysed Renaissance, Baroque and classical layouts and derived aesthetic principles which could be applied in future. He concentrated on plazas and established principles of proportion, visual sealing and monument location. Although he emphasized aesthetics, this was not because he thought they should be the sole criterion but in an effort to right the balance of goals, which he felt to incline excessively towards the technical. He was at pains to point out that 'the demands of art do not necessarily run contrary to the dictates of modern living (traffic, hygiene, etc.)' (Sitte 1965 p 92). Indeed some technical considerations originate in his book (though they may have been added by a follower). It is demonstrated that the T junction, which allows a layout with visual sealing, involves only three intersecting traffic trajectories whereas the crossroads, which is visually open, involves sixteen intersecting trajectories. He demonstrates the use of curved streets to avoid junctions at acute angles and to remove crossroads. Sitte also emphasizes the usefulness of visually-sealed layouts in preventing surface winds and the importance of aspect in making the best of the sun. Lastly, although his focus was primarily visual, he also stressed the important though obvious fact that the city is part of the experience of countless individuals. Only by considering those individuals can planners hope to produce a satisfactory human environment.

Sitte's ideas were adopted enthusiastically in northern Europe although shunned by the French. British acceptance was slower in coming but once Raymond Unwin and Patrick Geddes, the two foremost figures in British planning in the early years of the twentieth century, had taken up his ideas, his success was considerable. It is paradoxical that, although Sitte had focused almost exclusively on the layout of major buildings in city centres, his followers applied them to the design of developing areas on the city fringe.

If Camillo Sitte took inspiration from the past, other workers were inspired by future possibilities to create new urban forms. Arturo Soria y Mata had first proposed his linear city in 1882 and campaigned for its adoption for over thirty years with only minor success. The nub of the idea was that by building a city along a single train and trolley track all buildings could be adjacent to rapid transport and to the country. The old goals of functional efficiency, sanitation and amenity remain, but the physical form was dramatically new.

A second progressive direction was indicated by the work of Tony Garnier, *Une Cité Industrielle*, a detailed project completed in 1901. This work was chiefly remarkable for its anticipation of modern architecture, but also embodies some interesting features of layout. It exhibits a feature which was to become part of twentieth-century planning practice: rigid zoning to separate industry from residence. Other features are conventional: the residential area has a rectangular grid with public buildings in the centre. It is the form of the buildings which is most remarkable (Banham 1960 p 37). Pevsner remarks 'there are certain buildings in the Industrial City which appear to be wholly of today. For the first time here the possibility of misdating occurs' (Pevsner 1960, p 182). Garnier articulated the principle of functional architecture upon which his revolutionary designs were based: 'Truth alone is beautiful. In architecture, truth is the result of calculations made to satisfy known necessities with known materials' (Garnier 1917 p 98). Health, efficiency and a new form of aesthetic were the goals of Garnier's plan.

Planning activity in England was still bound up with the problems that had enmeshed it for the past half century and more. The Boer war had shown that a large proportion of potential recruits from the urban working class was unfit to serve and at least part of this was attributed to unhealthy urban environments (Ashworth 1954 p 168). Also suburban development was beginning to cover increasing areas of countryside with uncoordinated sprawl. The Housing, Town Planning, etc. Act of 1909 built on a number of more partial acts but concentrated on the regulation of suburban growth, which was expected to relieve pressure on central cities. The goals of the Act were to ensure 'proper sanitary conditions, amenity, and convenience in the laying out and use of the land . . .' (Section 54.1). As Ashworth puts it:

. . . Emphasis was no longer on the traditional advantages of the town, suitable provision for a wide variety of functions and activities in reasonable proximity, the physical conditions in which the stimulus of diverse and changing contacts are available to every inhabitant; it was on separation, on space rather than on what filled it, on trees, grass and gardens more than on shops, factories and pavements. (Ashworth 1954 p 187).

Unfortunately the provisions of the Act were optional, not mandatory, and the complex procedures envisaged deterred most local authorities from taking action. Such planning as did occur tended to be narrowly architectural in nature.

Perhaps the most significant planning activity in England at the turn of the century was the development of the Garden City movement from the theoretical stage into the practical. The history of the Garden City idea has been considered in detail in Unit 26, suffice it to say at this point that Ebenezer Howard had synthesized ideas from the model village tradition, the economist Henry George, Edward Bellamy and many other sources. His blue-print combined the best features of town and country and gave its inhabitants a measure of independence from landlords and employers by providing for municipal ownership of land and buildings. His coordinated treatment of all aspects of a sizeable settlement was a major step forward because before him, and for many years after the example had been set, official planning tended to be restricted to limited areas and some of the components of the city. Howard's goals included social justice, health, efficiency and contact with nature. Letchworth, laid out by Parker and Unwin added some of the aesthetic dimension introduced by Sitte.

SAQ 12   What new emphases had appeared by 1910 in the means of pursuing old goals?

3.3 Between the wars   In spite of legislation and the eventual success of Letchworth, urban development between the wars shows only one new feature: much lower densities. These occurred in the new suburban council estates, in planned and unplanned developments. These developments were permitted by improvements in transport, the electric underground train, tram, motor bus and motor car. The characteristic form of private housing was ribbon development of semi-detached houses, often with frontages on the arterial roads and by-passes which had made them possible. Local authority estates were recognizable by geometrical patterns and the mixture of short terraces with 'semis'. In the south industrial estates appeared in the new suburbs, but in the north stagnation and unemployment encouraged out-migration and limited new development. Slum clearance proceeded at a modest pace although between a quarter and a third of the housing in most large cities was thought to be unfit. During this period the town planning movement was in some disarray and, with the exception of Howard's second experiment, Welwyn Garden City, planning

Figure 9 Interwar ribbon development, Osterley (Aerofilms)

Figure 10 Interwar council estate, Liverpool (Aerofilms)

affected only a fraction of development and was insufficiently comprehensive when it did occur. Most planners seemed to have lost sight of their fundamental goals and to be concerned with details of layout.

Meanwhile, a comprehensive approach to city planning had been developed in Paris by Le Corbusier. His 'contemporary city', developed in the early 1920s, was based on an analysis of urban activity and growth and advocated a radical departure from current practice. The plan is underlain by an almost metaphysical devotion to the straight line and right angle, which he identifies with purpose and efficiency. The details of his scheme are presented in the Reader extract, which you are recommended to read.

The majority of the 3,000,000 inhabitants are housed in a number of garden cities beyond a protected zone of woods and fields. No detailed plans for these were presented. They were to be joined to the central city by rail and road. It is perhaps significant that what is likely to be the most human part of the city is not described: it gives us some insight into Le Corbusier's goals. Efficiency, rationalism and order are stressed throughout. The individual's satisfaction is not prominent – unless it be a single individual: the architect. 'The architect sees with pleasure that the notorious things we call "housing schemes" have been replaced by immense constructions on a noble scale' (Le Corbusier 1971 p 206).

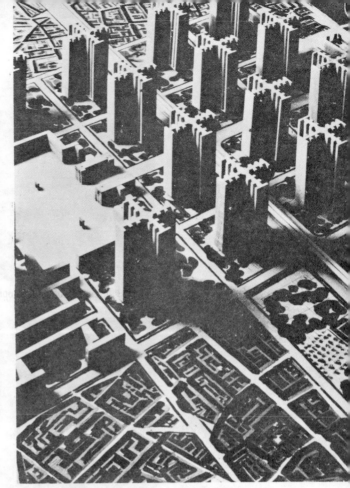

Figure 11a Unité d'Habitation, Marseilles
(J. Allan Cash)

Figure 11b Model of Le Corbusier's Plan Voisin for Paris, 1925
(Lucien Hervé)

One goal which seems absent is economy: the use of skyscrapers of sixty storeys in the absence of very high land rents was and is unprecedented, the use of half the volume of residential blocks as gardens is unlikely when most builders prefer economy even to small balconies. Even the chapter describing the financing of the Voisin plan to superimpose a new Business City of twenty-four skyscrapers on the centre of Paris was written without consulting an economist and uses the flimsiest of evidence – for example the multiplication of land values after Haussmann's surgery. It is worth noting that in prototype schemes which Le Corbusier actually built the departures from normal practice are smaller, for example the *Unité d'Habitation* block in Marseilles does have internal shopping and a running track on the roof but it does not have half its volume devoted to gardens.

On the other side of the Atlantic another visionary architect was developing ideas for a city of the future which was in many respects the antithesis of the 'contemporary city'. Broadacre city, developed by Frank Lloyd Wright, emphasized just those features of human life that Le Corbusier scorned. He believed that true human happiness resulted not from efficiency and material wealth alone but from contact with nature and people. This is not to say that Wright neglected technology; he was at least as aware of the importance of car, aeroplane and telephone as was Le Corbusier. The difference is that, as well as admitting such devices as means, he devoted a good deal of attention to the *ends* of urban development. In contrast to the 120 inhabitants per acre in the residential areas of the 'contemporary city', Broadacre city was to give an acre to each family. The non-residential activities, shops, employment and services, were to be decentralized but easily reached by the highways. His overall philosophy is encapsulated in one sentence. 'It will eliminate no modern comforts, yet it will keep the age-less health-giving comforts too' (Wright 1932 p 97).

The visions of Le Corbusier and Wright were probably too far ahead of their time to achieve wholesale adoption, though both have had far-reaching influence. A major stumbling block was that both seem to require a higher standard of living than is present even today: only a small proportion of the population can afford an acre of garden or one of Le Corbusier's spacious apartments. Their goals remain distant to most people even today.

A movement which originated in the same period and which became planning dogma for a time was that of the neighbourhood unit. Since this has been discussed in Unit 29, only a few remarks are needed here. One important feature of the neighbourhood unit was that, although not intended to do so by Perry, it suggested a physical form appropriate to a goal which was close to many planners' hearts: *community*. In accepting the fostering of a sense of community as a goal, planners had transcended the rather mundane desires for public health, structural soundness and functional efficiency and were beginning to prescribe for the higher things in life. The neighbourhood idea was both forward and backward looking. As Mumford points out (1966 pp 569–71), although cities had contained distinctive quarters from the earliest times, Perry was inspired to advance the neighbourhood concept by his observations of a wealthy suburb of New York. One may enquire whether the participation in cultural and political life he so admired was a result of social class or spatial layout. However, his ideas about design, including the provision of community centres, were taken up enthusiastically in many countries, including Britain, where they were incorporated into the design of the postwar New Towns (see Unit 29 Section 2).

SAQ 13   What were the two most radical changes in planning thought and practice between the wars?

3.4 The postwar years   The Second World War gave town planning a threefold impetus. First, there was widespread bomb damage to repair – for example, nine-tenths of the buildings in the then County of London were damaged to some extent. Second, the close national solidarity of the war years had produced a consensus in favour of more equality and social justice. Third, practical experience had shown that Government could plan and direct in fields which had been thought of as the preserve of private enterprise.

Apart from the numerous measures making up the Welfare State, two Acts were crucial to the emergence of a really effective planning system. The Distribution of Industry Act, 1945, gave the Government power to influence the location of industry, and with it the developments in housing and services. The Town and Country Planning Act, 1947, made planning an obligation of the county councils and made the process more complicated and more flexible.

The new goals of postwar British planning are summed up in the following quotations:

. . . Give a man and his wife a first rate house, a community, and occupation of various kinds reasonably near at hand, within a regional framework which allows them to move freely and safely about, to see their friends and enjoy the advantages of London; add to these a wide freedom of choice, and they will not grumble in the years immediately following the war. (Abercrombie 1945)

. . . What an impulse it will give to the solution of major problems of society if a great number of town dwellers secure the inalienable advantages of comfort in their houses, beauty and grace in their surroundings, sunlight, fresh air, health, and a share of civic power, if many more rural workers have access to the social pleasures and opportunities of lively towns, if to a greater extent people of all classes or functions in town and country are brought together and come to understand the interests of each other; then vital political issues will be immensely clarified and the rise of numerous groups of alert and responsible citizens will quicken national progress in every sphere. (Osborn 1942)

Ashworth (1954 p 235) confirms the change of emphasis which is apparent in the quotations from Abercrombie and Osborn: 'town planning was becoming concerned with the way people lived as well as with the way the buildings looked'. While the intentions may have been admirable, the amazing naivety of the suggestions that one can give people a community or bring different classes of people together in complete harmony must cast doubt on the means used, although they were better than ever before.

The rapid increase in the numbers of private motor vehicles faced planners with a new dilemma. Should they bow to the public's desire for car ownership and provide road space for private transport or should they limit cars and provide for adequate mobility by other means? The Buchanan Report on *Traffic in Towns* (1964) showed that it was literally impossible to cater for all urban transport by private car without destroying the majority of the central area of the city. Leicester, for example, would need an inner motorway of sixteen lanes by 1995. Buchanan's proposals were for a double compromise: much of the traffic would be diverted to public transport, though private cars would remain, and efficiency would be promoted by building main routes between 'environmental areas' which would be kept peaceful by the exclusion of all through traffic.

In deciding what should be done about urban transport Britain was able to profit from the experience and technical expertise of American planners. In other respects British planning has been more successful than its American counterpart. In the United States planners have had to operate in a society which has an almost religious regard for private enterprise. They have often had to work very closely with powerful institutions in order to get their plans implemented and as a result the plans have tended to reinforce the existing distribution of benefits in society. Gans (1968) shows that city planning in America started by adopting the goals of order and efficiency which white Anglo-Saxon Protestant elites had been using to try to minimize the impact of immigrants on the cities. Zoning, an important element of 'master planning', was supported by central-city business and affluent suburbanites because it favoured their economic and social interests. The neighbourhood idea was linked with anti-urban sentiments and encouraged segregation on class and race lines. City officials were usually closer to real estate developers' wish to maximize land values, and thus taxes, than to the inhabitants' desire for low rents.

Since the Second World War American planning has grown more effective, in that it has been widely implemented, but the flaws remain. Banfield (1968 pp 14–16) points out that efforts in the fields of transport and housing, which make up 90 per cent of Federal investment in the cities, have been contradictory but have on balance harmed the central city. Improved transport has allowed the mobile to move to the suburbs, thus reducing the urban tax-base. Subsidies and insurance for mortgages provided by the Federal Housing Administration have benefited the middle class and encouraged the flight to the suburbs. Urban renewal programmes, on the contrary, have tried to attract suburbanites back to a reconstructed central city – and displaced low income families in the process. Goodman (1972), who describes the miscarriages of the American system at great length, provides figures for the urban renewal process. 400,000 homes, mostly of low income people, have been demolished. They will be replaced by approximately half that number of new units and of these less than ten per cent will be public housing for the poor. Goodman's thesis that urban renewal was designed from the first as Federal subsidy for the real estate business is called into question by Gans's (1968 p 83) statement that it was precisely because of political opposition to public housing that the government sold cleared land to developers at prices a fraction of its market value. It appears that it was really the presence of a consensus among voters that planning should not redistribute wealth that ensured the miscarriage of urban renewal subsidies and not the military–industrial power elite blamed by Goodman. Experience in the United States indicates that, however much technical and theoretical expertise is available, planning cannot be successful in the absence of a political consensus about the goals to be pursued.

In Britain there appears to be general agreement that there should be planning – but no consensus as to what its goals should be. This ambivalent position is becoming obvious because many plans now have goals or objectives clearly stated at the outset (Unit 29 and Jackson 1971 Chapter 10). Where specific objectives are laid down, they almost always refer to the system level – for example that good agricultural land and land with mineral deposits should not be built over – and not to the individual level. Where objectives for individuals are laid down, they are usually in very general terms, stressing especially choice and mobility. Perhaps the most forthright statement comes from the Milton Keynes Development Corporation:

. . . From the beginning the Corporation has taken the view that the planning of the new city should be related to clear and explicit social goals. The Corporation intends that the Plan should describe and define the character of life which it is the new city's aim to provide and which the proposals are intended to achieve. This applies not only to the physical plan for the new city but to all the other proposals, social and economic. (MKDC 1970 p9)

Here is the firm commitment to planning. The six major goals, which have been discussed in Unit 29 are a good deal less firm.

Although goals such as those of the Milton Keynes plan require clarification if they are to be of any use in practice, for example by defining exact objectives in terms which can be assessed, it is reassuring to find practising planners emphasizing variety and freedom. We must, however, wait to see whether planned reality achieves their worthy goals.

One of the goals of Milton Keynes includes public participation. This has been the subject of much debate in professional and everyday journals. It has also been the subject of a government Report (the Skeffington Report) and Unit 22 of this course. Although public participation may seem to the unwary to be a self-evident good, there are considerable problems with the two forms of participation which are now common. Officially inspired participation takes the form of exhibitions, lectures and public enquiries. These are often ineffective devices since only a small minority of the public attend and few can read elaborate plans with sufficient facility to appreciate the effects of the plan on the ground. Any protest is immediately confronted by expert opinion and, at public enquiries, subject to cross-questioning by the lawyers of the planning authority. The process is, to say the least, poorly designed as a way of eliciting ideas and attitudes from the affected public. The second kind of participation occurs where pressure groups form to resist planning proposals. Recent examples have been the resistance to the Cublington airport and the slow progress

Figure 12 Covent Garden (Paul Smith)

of the M4 through commuter areas of Berkshire. The unfortunate aspect of this
form of participation is that it is almost always the wealthy and articulate
members of the middle class who are able to operate successfully in the intricate
web of the planning process. Successful defence of their interests usually results
in damage to the interests of poorer and less well educated people. This process
is commonplace in the USA: Julian Wolpert of the University of
Pennsylvania has investigated over 200 cases where freeways originally routed
through white middle class areas have been built through poor black areas.
This kind of participation may thus confound the ambition of many planners
to redistribute benefits to those in most need.

In spite of current difficulties there is no doubt that participation is an important
new goal for planning. It is the first goal that deals not with the outcomes of
the planning process but with the nature of the process itself. It will be one of the
important challenges to future planning to devise effective methods of
participation. In the absence of new procedures it may well occur that, as the
public and the media grow more aroused by environmental damage and more
conscious of their ability to obstruct plans, a diminishing proportion of plans
are implemented.

SAQ 14 In what way has the change in political atmosphere between the immediate
postwar years and the present day affected planners' ability to achieve their
goals?

3.5 Summary: goals of planning This brief survey of planning goals shows that the stated goals do not differ
greatly from those identified by the utopians. It is notable, however, that it has
been a good deal harder to achieve goals in reality than it is in fiction.

Planning goals at the individual level may also be divided into two groups.
'Freedoms from' include disease, bad housing, pollution, disorder and accident.
'Freedoms to' include participation in culture, community and the planning
process itself and centre very much on mobility and choice. Access to the
countryside, or at least green space and the experience of beauty are other
common goals.

Goals at the urban level centre upon the efficient use of resources, the
provision of a layout which maximizes access to desired facilities and minimizes
contact with nuisances, and sometimes include vaguer items like 'social
balance' or sense of community. In practice it is probable that most planners

do most of their thinking at the urban level rather than the individual level. It should, however, be borne in mind that the city was made for people and not people for the city.

Planning rarely makes explicit any goals at the societal level. However, at least three goals seem to be implicit. The adoption of public health measures in the face of cholera epidemics, the use of comprehensive planning in the two world wars and consideration of radical measures to avert the threatened ecological catastrophe indicate the highest level goal: survival. Threats to survival are probably the most effective way of inducing society to adopt radically new measures. The second goal at the societal level is to effect some degree of redistribution of real income and wealth. This may range from provision of a minimum welfare floor of 'freedoms from' to complete egalitarianism. The third goal is at a more pragmatic level: to perform those roles in society which free enterprise cannot. Essentially they focus on cases where customers cannot be identified and charged and where the scale of investment or degree of risk deter private capital. The use of public money to assure private contractors of an adequate return often involves planners in subsidy of the already wealthy and thus runs counter to the goal of redistribution.

Since any set of goals is likely to be partially inconsistent and because goals are often implicit or vaguely stated, it is difficult to assess to what degree planners have achieved their goals in this or any other country. At the broadest level it is clear that the combined activities of planning and the welfare state have failed to reduce the disparity between rich and poor, although they have prevented the gap from widening since the 1920s. In these circumstances it is not surprising to find that a minority of people have few of the basic 'freedoms from' while many have not only the minimum welfare floor, but also many of the freedoms to choose among a wide range of environments and facilities. Although there appears to be a reasonable level of overall efficiency in our towns and cities, the existence of a substantial minority of deprived individuals indicates that our society has not given adequate attention to its priorities.

In conclusion, two other points need to be made about the planning process. With the exception of the occasional large scheme, such as that of Haussmann, early planning tended to be partial and piecemeal. As time has passed planning powers have increased and planning techniques have become more refined. This trend towards increasing comprehensiveness seems likely to continue as long as the existence of social malfunctions shows that planning is not attaining even its initial goals. The second final point is that for most of its history planning has been attempting to bring obsolete environments up to date. As the pace of social and technical change increases this becomes increasingly inadequate. Future planning must increasingly design environments suited to the foreseeable future and sufficiently flexible to accommodate unexpected change.

SAQ 15   Consider any planned development with which you are familiar. First, list the goals of the scheme, explicit and implicit. Second, assess to what extent those goals are achievable in principle. Third, assess the degree to which they were achieved in practice and try to account for any inadequacies.

4 Future planning

It is clear from the survey in Section 3 and from looking at almost any daily newspaper that planning as presently conceived has a number of inadequacies. These involve what planners have failed to do, eg provide adequate housing for all – as well as the failings in what has been built, eg many planned developments are visually monotonous and some, especially high rise flats, unsuited for their purpose. These inadequacies have induced a number of people (Banham *et al* 1969) to advocate a complete abandonment of planning in three test areas of Britain. The illustrations in their article, which are mostly of commercial advertising, introduce the major problem in their argument, which was spelled out in the correspondence they stimulated: complete withdrawal of planning simply opens the way for commercial exploitation of the most profitable market. This reintroduces the inevitable adjuncts of the *laissez-faire* economy – increased social injustice and environmental ugliness as well as the vitality and freedom they sought. Although planning in the future may combine Government and free enterprise, their 'non-plan' does not appear to be the right combination.

An approach which is in many respects the antithesis of 'non-plan' was advanced in the *Ecologist*. This related to the highest level planning goal of all: survival. In essence their position is that pollution is disrupting ecological cycles on which we depend, population growth is outstripping food production and technological growth is exhausting resources. Although they cannot prove their contentions, it would be foolish to ignore the weight of evidence they can muster. In point of fact, even the most optimistic futurist agrees that something must be done: the difference between optimist and pessimist is whether it will be done in time. Reduction of pollution, population growth and resource extraction are likely to have a considerable effect on the form and life of the future city. The Ecologist's *A Blueprint for Survival* includes a programme of resettlement as well as profound industrial change (see the Reader extract). Although we may concur with the ecological principles they use, it is necessary to take issue with some of their more naive contraventions of social scientific wisdom. Perhaps the most notable problem is that the capital cost of resettling the four-fifths of the population who currently live in cities into villages would be prohibitive. The use of small manufacturing plants scattered all over the country would greatly magnify the problems of moving partly manufactured goods from plant to plant. The costs of reaching such a scattered market with manufactured products would outweigh the savings in distributing food. The strong social control and emphasis on status which is expected of these villages seems to be a deliberate recreation of some of the worst features of the traditional village. In fact many other patterns of settlement and forms of society may well go as far or further towards meeting the criteria for survival without the unfortunate consequence of the Blueprint. Most individuals given the choice seem to opt for a house with a large garden, so future densities are likely to fall. Concentration on self-development instead of consumption will shift emphasis from goods to services – a shift already occurring. Practices which endanger survival could be discouraged by taxation and vice versa. Thus, while it is necessary to monitor the situation constantly, survival seems possible for a society seeking higher goals. The problem is probably in deflecting today's materialist society from the illusion of indefinite growth. That will be a prime task in developing programmes to enable us to reach whatever goals society decides to be proper.

The two approaches we have outlined seem to miss the optimum in two directions: too little planning in 'non-plan' and too much in *A Blueprint for Survival*. A preferable approach would be to seek to improve the planning process as far as possible and to select complementary contributions to development with care. Such an approach should ideally be able to satisfy the goals of both variety and conservation, as well as many other goals neglected by 'non-plan' and *A Blueprint for Survival*.

Elimination of the current inadequacies of the planning process and the planned environment will require at least two developments. First, planners must be clearer about the goals they are pursuing. In a democracy this means that they must go to much greater lengths to identify public goals: planning must become more overtly political. Second, the technical and conceptual means of achieving these goals need further development. This more professional aspect of planning is largely beyond the scope of this course. The part of it which concerns this unit is how the planning process can attempt to satisfy everybody when different people have different goals. This is commonly stated as the goal of variety.

4.1 Political planning

Just as attitudes to past and present range from the irresistible force of the revolutionary to the immovable object of the reactionary, so attitudes to the future vary. Broadly speaking, the moderate may question whether the revolutionary ideal is possible, while accepting its desirability, or whether the reactionary ideal is desirable, while recognizing its feasibility. Most people are likely to give more favour to the two more moderate approaches named by Ewald (McCue and Ewald 1970 p 32) as *response* and *reason*. Response is probably the most influential political doctrine in this country and many others, though it has few formal adherents. Basically it involves a pragmatic obligation to rectify major problems and a willingness to make only such advances as are easily attainable. Reason involves a greater degree of idealism, in that it sets goals which may not be immediately attainable, but is sufficiently realistic to offer a programme by which those goals may be achieved. It is part of the thesis of this unit that planning in and for the future should progress beyond response into reason.

The survey of planners' goals shows that in practice a large proportion of planning effort has been a response to social and environmental problems. Although public health measures seem to be successful in the advanced countries, response to the lack of other 'freedoms from', especially in housing, are far from complete. In the developing countries provision of even the minimum 'freedoms from' are at an early stage. In the presence of so many problems which could be tackled on a response basis, it seems at first sight premature to recommend an immediate adoption of reason. However, this is not so. First, many people and areas are sufficiently prosperous that overt problems are not demanding a response from planners and, in the absence of goals for the future, it is not clear what developments ought to occur. Second, the adoption of a reasoning posture may show that simple response to symptoms may not be the best, or even an adequate way, of curing the malady. Planning as traditionally conceived deals with the built environment and attempts to eliminate undesirable features. Many of those features are, however, merely environmental outcomes of social processes. Slums are a case in point: the physical destruction of slums can achieve little if society contains a number of people who cannot afford to pay for decent housing. These people will merely relocate in the cheapest possible housing, and by overcrowding and under maintenance reduce it to a slum. The only effective way of removing slums is to increase the purchasing power of poor people. It may be argued that, in charging planners with the responsibility of removing slums while maintaining the social and economic systems that produce poor people who can afford to live nowhere else, governments have merely been using planners as scapegoats for their own inadequacy.

The lesson which emerges from this is that in future there should be an examination of planning goals to indicate which may be sensibly pursued through physical planning and which through other types of Government action. The provision of a reasonable minimum income is crucially important to any form of society, whether acting through free enterprise or planning, which is intending to use the mechanism of pricing and choice. If some people have inadequate resources, free choice is restricted and injustice inescapable. Taxation may affect not just individuals but also the institutions which affect the environment. For example a pollution tax which charged activities with the cost of repurification or of compensating the victims would be much more effective than the present system of fines. A general principle might be that every activity would be made responsible for what are now regarded as 'externalities' – by-products which are not relevant in optimizing the efficiency of the activity. Taxation could ensure that an activity was responsible for all its products which were relevant to society and environment and not just those it buys and sells in the market.

These ideas are developed in more detail by Webber (in Reader), which you should now read.

SAQ 16 In what way does a standard, as used by planners, differ:
a from engineering standards?
b from goals, as discussed in this unit?

SAQ 17 What two mechanisms does Webber discuss as possible ways of assessing public preferences for planning?

Although it seems likely that Webber's suggestion of pricing planning outputs would be more effective in indicating realistic public preferences than the political alternatives, it seems unlikely that a sufficiently adequate minimum income will be provided in the immediate future. During that immediate future the political alternatives are the only practical route to improvement. While planners' professional standards may be reasonably effective in providing the

Figure 13 Poster: Covent Garden
(Paul Smith)

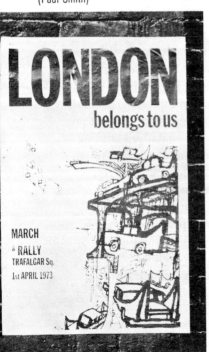

Figure 14 Bloomsbury participation poster
(Paul Smith)

basic 'freedoms from' one must accept the point made by Webber, Gans and others that planners have never been effective in providing for the less obvious needs of minorities. The issue of public participation also demonstrates the point. The inadequacies of participation as currently practised, which have been discussed above, show that some rethinking of the links between planning and the political process is needed.

The article by Rein (in Stewart 1972), which was required reading for Unit 29, discusses the sources of legitimacy available to American planners. You should refer to the article if you cannot remember its main outlines. Circumstances in Britain are rather different, because planning bodies are larger, better coordinated and armed with more effective statutory powers. The problem of legitimacy remains, however, and needs discussion. In a democratic society the presumption must be that the public is the final source of authority for planners. This introduces a paradox, in that planners, who are public servants supposedly representing the public interest, often find themselves in conflict with members of the public, and even whole communities. It is essential to consider what public is involved in what role.

The last word on planning matters rests with the Secretary of State for the Environment. He is a member of a national government elected, sometimes three or four years previously, on the basis of a number of highly generalized policies, hardly any of which explicitly recognize physical planning possibilities. The detailed planning activity is conducted by the local authorities. The councils which take the political initiatives are elected, often by a tiny minority of voters, after a campaign which focuses on national political issues and in which local planning issues have only minor influence. In these circumstances it is hard to see how the planners, who are often quite remote from political direction, can claim any public mandate for detailed programmes.

There would seem to be some trend towards inclusion of current planning schemes in council elections, for example, the issue of the motorway box seems to have played some part in the Labour victory in the 1973 GLC elections. However, there seem to be two problems. First, the complex dimensions of local planning options do not readily fit an arbitrary division into Conservative and Labour, but candidates from these parties enjoy a considerable advantage over independents in organization and publicity. Second, elections are a good deal rarer than planning issues. In spite of these problems, it would be a step in the right direction if candidates in local elections included detailed policies on development in their platform. Candidates should also be required to declare any financial interest in land or property, as such personal motivations could conceivably influence their receptiveness to public opinion.

Perhaps the most effective way of involving public preferences in the planning process which could be simply developed from current practice would be to hold referenda in the areas affected by planning proposals. There are already precedents for this, the Brighton marina being a case in point. There would appear to be two main problems inherent in this. First, the planning agencies would be subject to uncertainty and money spent on rejected plans would be wasted: the economic efficiency of planning would thus be reduced. Second, it is always hard to identify the relevant constituency: for example if a motorway is proposed between two cities it is likely to be supported by most of the motorists in those cities and indeed by the national Automobile Association but opposed by people whose gardens, farms and villages will be disrupted. In a democracy it is always assumed that the majority will prevail, but this becomes less straightforward when a minor improvement for the majority involves total disruption of the lives of the minority. The only resolution of this dilemma is probably the rethinking of the process of compulsory purchase and compensation. If those in favour of a development had to increase compensation sufficiently to reconcile those against, the inequity of planning projects could be reduced, if not eliminated.

Figure 15 Participation poster (Paul Smith)

The kinds of suggestion made in this section involve a greater blending of politics and planning. General planning policy should be incorporated into platforms at national and local elections and every attempt made to include public as well as ideological and bureaucratic goals in policy. Assessment of the means to be used, whether physical or legislative, requires dialogue between politicians and specialists, including planners, who are aware of the limitations of the effectiveness of the measures available. Public participation in drawing up detailed plans at the local level might well improve both the efficiency and the acceptability of the detailed proposals. Implementation of plans would involve consultation of those directly affected and financial adjustments to ensure that no individuals sustained an excessive amount of cost or benefit. Such modifications at the strategic level would ensure that public goals were incorporated into the planning process. However, as stated above, participation can only be just if power, which involves income and education, is more evenly distributed. The doubling or tripling of GNP *per capita* expected by 2000 will allow the complete elimination of poverty without reducing the income of the already affluent. A gradual redistribution is thus possible, but will only occur if pressure is applied to those who hold political power.

4.2 Planning for variety Most people would probably agree with the authors of non-plan that most planned environments are visually dull. In the short term people are often satisfied because they have moved from an old dwelling to a new house or flat. In the long run this relative satisfaction is liable to lessen and the problems become more obvious. Planning needs to anticipate the greater affluence of the future and produce environments with the virtues of the best spontaneous developments, whose variety often results from the actions of a number of designers and builders over a number of years, but without their vices – poor services, inconvenient layout and social divisiveness. The goal of variety is fundamental in allowing an increased freedom of choice.

Figure 16 Washington Mews, Greenwich Village (Camera Press)

The situation can clearly be improved to some extent even without the radical changes outlined in the last section. Large rises in the standard of living would reduce the importance of cost constraints and allow more scope for imagination. In some circumstances, especially holiday resorts where appearance is thought crucial, efforts have been made. While some of the new holiday villages on the Mediterranean have fallen into the trap of unsuccessful imitation, others, notably Port Grimaud near St Tropez, have succeeded in reconstructing much of the charm and variety of the best spontaneous settlements. Such projects tend to be expensive, although use of a computer can reduce labour inputs dramatically, but they seem a very roundabout way of achieving variety and can probably never simulate genuine spontaneity with total success. Also, since one man's charm is the next man's decadence, no single centralized approach can satisfy everybody. The problem is to seek methods which may satisfy some people rather than opting for the mediocre on the grounds that it offends the smallest number.

Reference to systems theory shows that this practical difficulty is also a theoretical one. The Law of Requisite Variety states that 'to control a system of given variety we must match it with a controlling system of requisite variety' (Chadwick 1971 p 71). Chadwick's final summary of the systems approach to planning emphasizes that cities differ from engineering systems

Figure 17 Habitat '67: designed variety (Peter Mitchell/Camera Press)

in two ways: they are vastly more complicated and they contain self-determining individuals. For this reason they cannot be entirely controlled except by a tyranny which suppresses variety to a manageable level. The nature of individuals and institutions does, however, mean that they have the capacity to control themselves to a considerable degree. The planners can thus confine themselves to dealing with parts of the system knowing that the parts of it that they neglect will run themselves, although not always exactly as the planners would. The role of removing malfunction and preventing future ruin would appear to be the planners' proper role and the provision of variety, spontaneity and higher goals like community and self-actualization the prerogative of the populace. In most areas of society this is in fact the case, in societies which range from capitalist to communist. But in the case of the built environment, building regulations have developed into partly unnecessary sets of petty restrictions.

This argument supports the case put by Webber in the Reader. The relevant conclusion is that planning should adopt some means of measuring its *output*, not just its input, and that in many cases this can be based on pricing. The income of the offered facilities would show the amount of need for each and thus guide future investment decisions. He stresses, however, the need to take action about the distribution of income and wealth *before* pricing systems can justly be used. This, and other measures to which he shows pricing is impossible, must be determined in the political arena.

Alexander, in the Reader, takes the proposition for a 'framework' planning a step further by showing how physical forms can be designed to fit human needs. Although not stipulated in his paper, it is clear that different bodies could be responsible for building different facilities. The road network should be the direct responsibility of planners but other features could be delegated. Construction of schools and city hall would be a function of the local authority, places of employment of business, after the planners have checked that the proposed activity was compatible with the location, eg that polluting activities would not be placed in a residential area. Houses could be built by their occupants as individuals or as groups with a common interest, eg space for their children to play. One can see how planners could sketch the outlines and maintain supervision while delegating the detail to those more closely concerned. A greater interest by prospective occupants could save many of the problems which have been seen in the past: it is for example doubtful that many families would press for the construction of tower blocks – especially if incomes allowed an element of free choice.

The establishment of a social system and planning process in which officials ensured the basic 'freedoms from' and coordinated networks of transport and communications would provide the circumstances in which higher goals could be achieved. Haworth (1970) has explored the nature of 'the good city' at length. He believes that it is a city which allows maximum room for self realization and development. Self realization requires contact with both the good and the right. Historically right, involving duty, has been associated with community while good, involving individual opportunity, has been associated with modern society. Haworth believes that the benefits of community and opportunity can and should be combined in the future. Such a city would be rich, open and person-centred. Community would be encouraged by a greater degree of shared values (which would incidentally be likely if the range of income were narrower) but participation in it would be voluntary. Unlike traditional communities, it would not be inward looking or involve enmity to outsiders. It seems, in fact, to bear a considerable relation to what Gans (1968) called the community of limited liability, currently to be found in suburban areas in the USA, except that Haworth stipulates that in order for people to identify with an institution, whether community or workplace, the purpose of that institution must be good, a condition which is not obviously satisfied in areas incorporated to keep rates low and Negroes out or in companies devoted to making a profit, often from the manufacture of futile or destructive devices.

Sennett (1973) draws a parallel between the psychological process whereby adolescents, overwhelmed by the complexity of their emerging character, set up very rigid definitions of themselves and others in order to achieve simplicity through an act of faith, and adults migrating to a suburb where urban complexity can be replaced by homogeneous tranquillity. In turn these are related to the planners, attempt to separate urban functions and to replace varied spontaneous developments by worthy but monotonous estates. The consequences at the individual level are a failure to achieve self knowledge and a self-imposed restriction of capacity. At the urban level active communities are replaced by areas filled by individuals who have contact with only a few of their neighbours. The city becomes machine-like instead of being more complex than any organism.

Sennett proposes that the unfortunate trends in individual and social behaviour in cities could be reversed by reducing the legal and bureaucratic controls. This would require people to negotiate with their potential enemies and form active alliances with friends. In the process, individuals would increase their awareness of self and others and an active heterogeneous community would emerge. Through the experience of a low level of disorder and conflict, people would become more able to react appropriately to serious disorder, if it ever threatened. In brief then, his case is that the goals of variety, community and self actualization are more likely to be achieved by a reduction in the amount of planning than by an increase.

This should not be taken as an exact resurgence of the theme of 'non-plan', although a partial overlap exists. The argument that some goals for urban development may best be achieved by less physical planning does not extend to the more strategic level of planning where assessment of future needs and constraints, creation of possible programmes and provision of needed systems for sanitation, transport, communications and other utilities will still require the technical expertise of planners.

5 Conclusion

The greater part of this unit has concentrated upon one of the two traditions in city planning recognized by Webber – social reform. The second, the engineering tradition, has received only incidental attention. This is because the social reform tradition provided many of the fundamental goals for urban improvement while the engineering tradition provided the means for attaining some of them, notably health and urban transport. As a result of this focus it has been necessary to consider policy at the societal level where a more traditional discussion might have looked only at the urban level. However, in order to avoid over-abstraction and ideological rhetoric, an attempt has been made to focus on the way urban and societal systems impinge on individuals. It would seem unexceptionable that individuals should be freed from want and given freedom to choose among a variety of life styles and environments. The future perspective taken in this block suggests that this aim could easily be achieved by the year 2000 in this country and most of the present developed world. The prospects for the third world are not so optimistic unless means are found to provide really effective aid.

The Reader article by Mumford stresses that the city has seen the opposition of two sets of forces throughout its history. On the one hand it has encouraged the development of freedom, self development and originality and on the other it has allowed the establishment of repression and coercion on an unprecedented scale. Present-day cities exhibit signs of both syndromes. Although one hopes that future cities will be typified by an increasing proportion of the former, this will not come about spontaneously but will require a conscious effort by the citizens of the future to manifest their political power and keep in check the institutions which unnecessarily restrict their freedom. In spite of the protestations of revolutionaries and reactionaries this struggle will in all probability be waged mainly with words and ideas. The achievement of a truly democratic open future depends on the participation of concerned people in thinking about the future. Since the future is not just an academic topic but *your* future, I hope you may be moved to participate actively yourself.

Answers to SAQs

Answer SAQ 1   'Proper health' seems to overlap all others. Guarantee of food, clothes, shelter and medical care ensures at least an adequate material standard and thus removes obstacles to health. Leisure activities are only permitted if they are not injurious to proper health – but the concept includes moral prohibitions, eg of adultery, as well as those, like drinking, which might be injurious to physical health.

Answer SAQ 2   There seems to be an interesting mixture of efficiency and charity. Internally, the central administration ensure efficiency in assembling Utopia's surplus. Externally, charity appears in the gift of one-seventh to the poor, but efficiency in the use of six-sevenths to finance wars. Efficiency ensures success in war, but the purposes of war include charity – freeing their neighbours from tyranny – as well as self-help in punishing foreigners for unsatisfactory treatment of Utopian merchants.

Answer SAQ 3   Although the material standard of living seems hardly generous, it does seem adequate. The lack of freedom to choose one's own activities and life style is more serious: Utopia is by most standards a dull place and there is considerable doubt whether it would provide a satisfying environment for most people. It is curious that More should have sought to eliminate the possibility of vice without considering that this might also involve the elimination of virtue and the unnecessary limitation of pleasure. In the supposed absence of religious authority, there seems to be no adequate source of definition of vice. In general, Utopia appears rather negative: emphasis is on what may not be done and not on what might be.

Answer SAQ 4   Self-respect, consideration for others and good health. The first two are pursued for altruistic reasons, the last because of the strong social and legal pressure against illness.

Answer SAQ 5   At the urban level we are told little – although the towns are described in passing as beautiful. The major goal which is revealed at the societal level is implicit in the banning of machines. This suggests a determination to keep society human. However, what the humans are to occupy themselves with is not stated, although there are a few references to the existence of a conventional business system with great honour as the reward of financial success.

Answer SAQ 6   First the guarantee of freedom from any material deprivation, absolute or relative, by giving all the same large credit. Second, the guarantee of freedom to choose recreational activities and way of life, providing one's labour service is satisfactorily performed.

Answer SAQ 7   Housing is everywhere adequate. Public buildings are numerous and streets efficient, as is the system of pneumatic tubes for delivering goods. Public events are frequent.

Answer SAQ 8   Although there is a concern for efficiency in the conduct of the industrial army, this does not seem to be an end in itself. It is the means of maximizing the output from a given amount of labour and thus maximizing the credit to individuals.

Answer SAQ 9   Complete freedom from want and constraint, a good social life and artistic satisfaction in work.

Answer SAQ 10   The Mote of parish, ward or commune. This coordinates maintenance and development of the physical environment – but works only with volunteer labour, so minimizes constraint on individuals.

Answer SAQ 11   The public health movement seems to be an example of provision of one of the basic 'freedoms from' – in this case freedom from epidemic diseases. The motivation may perhaps be different: whereas the utopians provided 'freedoms from' in deference to the principles of social justice, the Victorians accepted sanitary reform partly to prevent the wealthier people from threats of infection by disease from the slums.

The emphasis on urban transport has no parallel in the works we have surveyed, although it does occur in utopian literature, for example in the work of H. G. Wells. It is noteworthy that, while it might be interpreted as a desire to give individuals freedom of mobility, in practice it was conceived as a wish to link large cities into functional wholes. This is an example of a planning goal at the city level, effectively abstracted from its effects on individuals.

The minor goal of preservation of public order is of interest not just because it indicates the wide divisions in nineteenth century society but because, where More treated the *causes* of disorder – deprivation and the existence of a 'culture of poverty' – Haussmann prepared in his plan to treat the *effects* in the form of active riots.

The fact that attempts to provide improved working class housing, as opposed to destruction of slums, were confined to philanthropists, shows that at that time there was no consensus among those who wielded power that there was any need for planning to redistribute costs and benefits. Increased efficiency and the preservation of vested interests were the main features of this early planning.

Answer SAQ 12   The goal of *public health* was still much discussed. However, the emphasis was more on low density, and access to open space than on sewage systems. The style of Haussmann was more in evidence than that of Chadwick, probably because sewers were commonplace in new developments.

Concern over *urban transport* had grown. It was now involving the development of new layouts as well as improving the vehicles and routes. At an individual level this improved convenience. At the urban level it increased efficiency.

Pursuit of *social justice* had taken a radical step. Earlier, philanthropists either had to operate in the difficult conditions of the urban land market or establish villages which they completely dominated. The establishment of Letchworth, although it used private capital, showed that municipal ownership could ensure standards and reduce rents without imposing personal subservience.

Overall, there was a new emphasis on the way developments were laid out. The disparate goals of efficiency, health, amenity and aesthetics could all be sought in a single layout. At that time there was no attempt to use layout to improve social justice, indeed in the US zoning was beginning to be used to reduce social justice by limiting areas of poor housing so that densities and prices rose and by zoning industry near poor housing and far from the homes of the wealthy and powerful.

Answer SAQ 13   The work of Frank Lloyd Wright and Le Corbusier showed that pursuit of the old goals of efficiency and contact with open space might require radically new urban forms, but this was not as great a change as the adoption of the creation of community as a planning goal. Here planners were beginning to go beyond provision of 'freedoms from' and functional efficiency to attempt to impose a particular style of life. It is fortunate in this instance that the causal effects of the physical environment are so weak that in effect planners could at most increase the opportunity for the development of community if it was chosen by the residents.

Answer SAQ 14   The war had produced a great degree of national solidarity and a consensus that the costs and benefits of life should be more equally distributed. Planning was in good repute because it was associated with the organization of the successful war effort.

Today the consensus for equalization seems almost absent, partly because absolute standards have risen, partly because many people erroneously believe that a measure of equalization has been achieved. Planning has become a dirty word associated with loss of individual freedom and destruction of valued environments.

In these circumstances planners face considerably increased opposition since pressure groups arise to fight almost any proposal. The existence of vocal opposition groups undermines public confidence in the legitimacy of planning because if planners go ahead they appear to be steamrollering the little men and if they change their plans seem to be vacillating and arbitrary. The crucial need is thus for some means whereby planners can be seen to enjoy public support.

Answer SAQ 15   Compare your answer with Section 3, 'Planning goals'.

Answer SAQ 16   An engineering standard involves three elements: a goal (eg a beam to span a given gap and support a given load), relevant theory relating dimensions to behaviour (in our example strength), and practical experience of successful application of the theory. Planning standards are not often supported by empirically validated theory, and can rarely draw on experience in exactly analogous situations. The relations between planning standards and goals is not always clear. Standards ought to be measurable objectives linked clearly to general goals. The lack of a clear link means that attainment of standards may often be irrelevant to the explicit or implicit goals behind them.

Answer SAQ 17   The market place and the political arena. Use of the market place, through pricing the products of planning, can only be just if all have an adequate income to exercise choice.

References   ABERCROMBIE, P. (1945) *Greater London Plan, 1944*, London, HMSO.

ALEXANDER, C. (1969) 'Major changes in environmental form required by social and psychological demands' in *Ekistics*, 28, pp 78–85.

ASHWORTH, W. (1954) *The Genesis of Modern British Town Planning*, London, Routledge and Kegan Paul.

BANFIELD, E. (1968) *The unheavenly city*, Boston, Little Brown and Co.

BANHAM, R. (1960) *Theory and design in the first machine age*, London, Architectural Press.

BANHAM, R. *et al* (1969) 'Non-plan: an experiment in freedom' in *New Society*, 20 March, pp 435–43.

BELLAMY, E. (1890) *Looking Backward 2000–1887*, Boston, Houghton Mifflin.

BUCHANAN, C. (1964) *Traffic in Towns*, Harmondsworth, Penguin Books.

BUTLER, S. (1970) *Erewhon*, Harmondsworth, Penguin Books.

CHADWICK, G. (1971) *A systems view of planning*, Oxford, Pergamon Press.

CHOAY, F. (1972) *The modern city: planning in the 19th century* (translated by HUGO, MARGUERITE and COLLINS, G. R.) London, Studio Vista.

ECOLOGIST (1972) *A blueprint for survival*, Harmondsworth, Penguin Books.

FOURIER, C. (1849) *Cités ouvrières. Des modifications à introduire dans l'architecture des villes*, Paris, Libraire phalansterienne.

GANS, H. J. (1968) *People and Plans*, Harmondsworth, Penguin Books.

GARNIER, T. (1917) *Une cité industrielle: étude pour la construction des villes*, Paris, Vincent.

GOODEY, B. (1970) 'Mapping Utopia', *Geographical Review*, 10, 1, pp 15–30.

GOODMAN, R. (1972) *After the planners*, Harmondsworth, Penguin Books.

HAWORTH, L. (1970) *The Good City*, Bloomington and London, Indiana University Press.

HUXLEY, A. (1932) *Brave New World*, London, Chatto and Windus.

HUXLEY, J. (1960) 'The emergence of Darwinism' in TAX, S. (ed) (1960) *The evolution of life. Its Origins, History and Future*, Chicago, Chicago University Press.

JACKSON, J. N. (1971) *The Urban Future*, London, Allen and Unwin.

LE CORBUSIER (1971) *The city of tomorrow*, (translated by F. ETCHELLS from *Urbanisme*, first published 1929) London, The Architectural Press.

MANUEL, F. (1965)' Towards a psychological history of utopias' in *Daedalus*, 94, pp 293–322.

MCCUE, G., EWALD, W. and MIDLAND RESEARCH INSTITUTE (1970) *Creating the Human Environment*, Urbana, University of Illinois Press.

MEYERSON, M. (1961) 'Utopian traditions and the planning of cities' in *Daedalus*, 90, pp 180–93.

MILTON KEYNES DEVELOPMENT CORPORATION (1970) *The Plan for Milton Keynes*, Vol 1, Wavendon, MKDC.

MINISTRY OF HOUSING AND LOCAL GOVERNMENT (1969) *People and Planning: Report of the committee on public participation in planning* (Skeffington Report) London, HMSO.

MORE, T. (1910) *Utopia*, London, Dent (first published 1516).

MORRIS, W. (1891) *News from nowhere*, London, Reeves and Turner.

MUMFORD, L. (1966) *The city in history*, Harmondsworth, Penguin Books.

ORWELL, G. (1949) *1984*, London, Secker and Warburg.

OSBORN, F. (1942) *New towns after the war*, London, J. M. Dent.

PEVSNER, N. (1960) *Pioneers of Modern Design*, Harmondsworth, Penguin Books.

REIN, M. (1969) 'Social planning: the search for legitimacy' in *Journal of the American Institute of Planners*, 35, pp 233–44 (also in STEWART 1972).

SENNETT, R. (1973) *The uses of disorder: personal identity and city life*, Harmondsworth, Penguin Books.

SITTE, C. (1965) *City planning according to artistic principles*. Trans. by G. R. and C. C. Collins. New York: Random House.

SORIA Y MATA, A. (1894) *La ciudad lineal, antecedentes y varios acerca de su contruccion*, Madrid, Est Tipografico 'Successores de Rivadenegra'.

STEWART, M. (1972) *The city: problems of planning*, Harmondsworth, Penguin Books (set book).

TEILHARD DE CHARDIN, P. (1959) *The Phenomenon of Man*, New York, Harper.

WEBBER, M. (1969) 'Planning in an environment of change. Part II Permissive planning' in *Town Planning Review*, pp 277–95.

WRIGHT, F. L. (1932) *The disappearing city*, New York, W. F. Payson.

Acknowledgements   Grateful acknowledgement is made to the following sources for illustrations used in this unit:

Figure 1: The Masters and Fellows of Trinity College, Cambridge; *Figures 2, 3, and 4:* Reproduced with the permission of the University of London Library; *Figures 5, 9, 10 and part cover:* Aerofilms; *Figure 6:* London Transport Executive; *Figure 7:* Courtesy of the Peabody Trust; *Figure 8:* Courtesy of the Guinness Trust; *Figure 11a:* J. Allan Cash; *Figure 11b:* Lucien Hervé; *Figures 12, 13, 14 and 15:* Paul Smith; *Figure 16:* Camera Press; *Figure 17:* Peter Mitchell/Camera Press.

Unit 33 The demise of the city ?
Andrew Blowers

Contents Unit 33

The demise of the city?

Aims The aims of this unit are:
1 To consider the future of the city:
  a as a distinctive spatial form;
  b as a distinctive form of social organization;
  c in the context of society as a whole.
This aim will be approached from the viewpoint of western societies, though some indication is given of the potential of urban development elsewhere.
2 To examine the major problems that will confront the future society and the scope for their solution.
3 To identify the major goals of the future society and the means for their attainment.

Objectives After reading this unit you should be able to:
1 Understand the following terms: social scale, inclusive spatial group, exclusive membership group, exponential growth, 'doubling time', and stable society.
2 Indicate differences between urban development in western USA and that in the rest of the affluent western world.
3 Understand what is meant by increasing social and spatial scale and the factors responsible for them.
4 Assess the implications for urban development of increasing spatial and social scale.
5 Discuss the role of small scale communities in future urban development.
6 Consider the relevance of the city to the study and selection of the major problems of society.
7 Indicate the future of society if present trends continue inexorably.
8 Examine the alternative to the demise of society.
9 Suggest the changes in social goals that might occur in a stable society.
This unit covers a broad and speculative field. Consequently you will only be able to satisfy these objectives in general terms. The self-assessment questions are designed to encourage you to think about the nature of the issues involved rather than to become immersed in detail.

Reading guide There are four articles in the set books which are *required reading* for this unit. The first pair are primarily concerned with the concept of increasing scale and its consequences, the second with the city in relation to the environment and society as a whole.

1 Greer, Scott (1962) 'The changing image of the city', Chapter 7 of *The emerging city*, The Free Press, New York (in the Reader).
This is the final part of a book which examines the changing nature of American urban society. Greer is especially concerned with the increasing scale of society which is causing the decline of the traditional city with its central area and localized communities. This extract provides a useful background to Section 2 of the unit which deals with the concept of increasing scale.

2 Webber, Melvin M. (1968) 'The post-city age', *Daedalus*, Journal of American Academy of Arts and Sciences, 97, 4, pp 1,092–9 (in Bourne, L. S. (ed) (1971) *Internal structure of the city*, pp 496–501).
This paper identifies three major themes which are familiar in much of Webber's work. First, that increasing scale is leading to the demise of the city; second, that it is important to distinguish between social and spatial scale; and third, that many urban problems have their origin in society and cannot be solved within the existing urban administrative framework. All three themes are taken up in this unit.

3 Ecologist (1972) 'Creating a new social system' from *A blueprint for survival*, first published in *The Ecologist*, 2, 1, 1972, revised edition published by Penguin Books (in the Reader).

This piece is recommended reading for Unit 30 and, with the piece by Ward and Dubos (see below) should be read in conjunction with Section 2 of this unit. The issue of human survival is central to this polemic. The impending doom of mankind can only be avoided by the creation of a stable society.
The extract discusses the new social system organized around the small community that will be necessary to ensure the goals of *community feeling* and *global awareness* essential to survival.

4 Ward, Barbara and Dubos, Renée (1972) *Only one earth*, Penguin books (in the Reader).

This extract is from a wide-ranging and unsentimental survey of the potential environmental crisis facing the world. It focuses on the problems of cities and the impact of the built environment upon individuals. The need for human identity in the small scale community is emphasized.

There are, in addition, other readings which we *recommend* you to read for the impression they give of what it might be like to live in the future urban society:

1 Hall, Peter (1969) 'The Dumills' in *London: 2000*, London, Faber and Faber, pp 268–73 (in the Reader).

2 Leicester, Colin (1970) 'Life in the year 2000 AD' in MacArthur, Brian (ed) (1970) *New horizons for education*, Council for Educational Advance (in the Reader).

These are two personalized extracts depicting daily life in the year 2000. Hall's account of the Dumill family illustrates how greater mobility and affluence may encourage much wider spatial horizons in the expanding metropolis. Everybrit, in Leicester's essay, inhabits a world in which technology has eliminated many routine and time-consuming operations. Work is a less central activity and the use of leisure assumes considerable importance.

3 Davie, Michael (1972) 'The end of the city' from *In the future now*, Chapter 4, pp 72–83.

The future city, at least in western societies, is arguably already present in Los Angeles. 'The need for a city in California is, quite simply, disappearing, replaced by the dispersed suburban life based on mobility and social exclusiveness, a safe and beautiful rest-home, cut out from the pain of the world, for healthy people.'

4 Ballard, J. G. (1966) *Billennium*, in Knight, D. (ed) *Cities of Wonder*, Sphere Books edition 1970.

This apparently light hearted account of life in a teeming city of the future conveys an impression of the deterioration in the quality of life that might occur if present population trends continue inexorably.

5 Simak, Clifford (1952) *City*, Weidenfeld and Nicolson; Science Fiction Book Club 1961 (in the Reader).

Simak's book consists of a series of myths handed down to the Dogs who have succeeded the human race on the earth. In this extract which is set in the twenty-first and twenty-second centuries man abandons the city but retains his need for a 'huddling place'.

6 Huxley, Aldous (1967) *Brave New World*, Chapter 5 (in the Reader).

7 Forster, E. M. (1928) 'The machine stops' in *The eternal moment and other stories*, London, Sidgwick and Jackson.

Forebodings about the nature of the future society are expressed in the two literary excerpts by Huxley and Forster. *Brave New World* is a stratified, segregated society in which people are conditioned to the conformity imposed by a benevolent but totalitarian regime. The excerpt illustrates how the power elite uses drugs and synthetic amusements to divert the attention even of the most privileged class from their position of powerless subjection.

In Forster's narrative man's dependence on the technology he has created is absolute. The world is one vast subterranean city inhabited by people living alone in individual cells in frequent but futile communication through the Machine. Visits to the surface are rare and personal contact is shunned. Social control is exercised by the Machine and when the Machine fails, humanity, too, is doomed.

1 Introduction

'Soon, London will be all England' (James 1, quoted by Wrigley, Unit 1)

Attempts to forecast, anticipate, and direct the future of the city accept implicitly that there is an *urban* future to speculate about. The theme of this course, indeed its central assumption, has been that there is such a phenomenon as the city and a process of urban development. It may be difficult to give precision to the definition of urban concepts[1] or to apprehend the interaction of urban subsystems and their interrelationship within the urban system, or to predict the implications of planning policies. But we have not questioned that it is worth doing all of these in order to understand and organize urban society. In this unit we ask, simply, has the process of urban development proceeded so far that it will no longer be worthwhile or relevant to isolate the city as a focus of study ? Are we experiencing now or can we foresee in the future, the demise of the city ?

It will be clear from the course that 'city' and 'urban' are terms that have many connotations. A city may be conceived as a spatial, economic, or social system. Each of these systems is related to larger national, or international systems, or to smaller internal subsystems of individual cities. Each system interacts with others but they do not, necessarily, occupy the same territory. Unit 7 demonstrated how the spatial and social aspects of the neighbourhood concept are complementary but not coincident. When we speak of the demise of the city we must be clear as to our terms of reference. Although the social and economic processes of urban development tend to be interdependent and are manifest in particular forms of spatial organization, for the purposes of analysis we should be aware of their separate identity.

Despite changes in physical appearance and life styles, urban forms and urban society retain distinct and distinguishable characteristics. Wirth's tripartite definition of the city in terms of its size, density and heterogeneity still appears to apply in many parts of the world. But the changes that have occurred in certain areas (notably the western USA) are such that the urban and non-urban are becoming indistinguishable, at least for some social groups. There the affluent mobile society inhabiting the 'non-place urban realm' (Unit 31) already exists according to some (see Davie in Reader and also Webber in Unit 18, pp 133–7). Whether the trend perceived in California will penetrate all levels of society and all cultural groups and be diffused across the world is a matter for speculation. It is possible to argue that there is an inexorable

---

1 See, for example, Hamnett 'What is a City?' Block 1 Supplementary Material, and Unit 7, 'The neighbourhood: exploration of a concept'.

trend towards increasing scale in American society that could be repeated, after varying intervals of time, elsewhere in the world. We shall now examine the evidence for this prediction.

SAQ 1   What are the distinguishing characteristics of urban development in western USA?

2 The concept of increasing scale

... Such a society might be larger in scale than any we can conceive today, and its way of life might be described as 'urbane' if not urban, but settlement would be freed from spatial limitations and the city would be no more. (Greer 1962 p 206; in Reader) ... We still talk of the city but have long gone beyond it. The most persuasive current estimates suggest that what we call the city is being overtaken by something grander, more complex, different in essence and scale. (Keller 1972 p 592)

The prediction that the city may disappear in the future both as a discrete physical entity and as a distinct socio-economic system arises from two parallel and, to some extent, reciprocal trends. One is the increasing spatial scale of cities as they expand outwards and as the process of *urbanization* engulfs more and more of the rural hinterland (Units 23 and 24). The other is the increase in social scale whereby *urbanism* is becoming the way of life of the whole society.

2.1 Increasing spatial scale

Various concepts have been invented to describe the increasing spatial scale of cities. *Metropolis* (Unit 23) has become *megalopolis* (Unit 31) and *ecumenopolis* (Unit 31) represents the demise of the independent city. Already in the most advanced countries the urban population, however defined, exceeds well over half the population. In Britain it has long been more than four-fifths of the total. Planning restrictions in Britain have contained the spread of cities and preserved a fairly clear distinction between urban and rural. In the process green belts have been established to mark the limits of expansion and to provide recreational areas for the urban population, and new towns have been established both as satellites and growth points. The growth of existing towns and the spread of settlement within the rural exurban areas is also subject to considerable control.

In the USA the spatial diffusion of cities has been more spontaneous and has been variously interpreted. These interpretations have been considered in Unit 31 from the viewpoint of changing urban form. Here I am primarily concerned with the implication of changing form. Friedman and Miller (1965; in Reader) expect the existing relationship of dominance and dependency between urban and rural to be transcended. The areas outside the standard metropolitan statistical areas (SMSAs – for definition see Unit 23) but within a hundred miles of them, which they define as the 'urban field' will experience rapid growth and relinquish their economic and social distinctiveness:

... The United States is becoming a thoroughly urbanized society, perhaps the first such society in history. The corresponding view of a city is no longer of a physical entity, but of a pattern of point locations and connecting flows of people, information, money, and commodities. (Friedman and Miller 1965)

They are aware of the economic and social forces behind this urban spread but feel that it will be confined to the urban field. Berry (1970) goes further predicting that even areas remote from existing cities will become involved in the urbanization process. He even speculates that these areas may become the future centres of innovation and growth thus acquiring one of the traditional roles of the urban centres.

Wolf (1969) interprets the process quite differently. Like Friedman and Miller he takes a quotation from Don Martindale's Introduction to Max Weber's *The City* (1958): 'The modern city is losing its external and formal structure. Internally it is in a state of decay while the new community represented by the nation everywhere grows at its expense. The age of the city seems to be at an end.' Wolf, however, denies that 'the demise of a spatial form or structure' is being witnessed in urbanized America. He uses the concept of the metropolitan tidal wave first introduced by Blumenfeld (see Unit 31 and the paper by Boyce in Bourne 1971). This gives a dynamic expression to population growth and movement in major cities analogous to a tidal wave moving outwards from the centre. Growth is most vigorous at the crest while behind in the inner city zone growth slows down and may eventually decline (rather like a recession wave). In front of the zone not yet reached by the advancing crest, growth increases and land is in a transitional stage between agricultural and urban uses (similar to a precession wave). Wolf applies this idea, with modifications, to Ohio (Figure 1; see also Unit 31 Table 1) where the speed of the tidal wave has increased from a mile per decade at the beginning of the century to about three miles by mid-century. During this period the shape of the wave has been modified to take into account changes in population density and the expansion outwards of the urbanized area. He suggests that there is a 'dialectical process' of attraction (centralization) and repulsion (diffusion) of population in which the centrifugal forces remain dominant and the city continues its outward spread. But while the process has remained consistent the scale has altered as the zone of growth has moved outwards especially with the advent of greater personal mobility. 'The basic form or structure remains; its magnitude is greater and its compaction less' (Wolf 1969 p 142).

Figure 1 New York Freeway. Mobility has freed people from their dependence upon localized communities. The divide between urban and rural is no longer clear as freeways link together dispersed developments Source: USIS

Whatever the interpretation of the spatial aspect of increasing scale it is motivated by a desire for more space and amenity and made possible by the increase in mobility. Increasing personal mobility is, in part, the result of rising car ownership. Davie (in Reader) believes this will be largely responsible for the future demise of the city:

... the car ... is the essential passport to a mode of living in which the city, as traditionally conceived, has little, if any, place: the car is the main technological item that is making the city out of date and prefiguring the end of the city altogether. (Davie 1972 p 74)

There is no doubt that, for some people at least, personal mobility has overcome distance constraints and reduced dependence on locality. The implications of this are reiterated time and again by writers such as Webber: 'The physical boundaries of settlements are disappearing, and the networks of interdependence are becoming functionally intricate and spatially widespread' (Webber 1963 p 24).

Not everyone, even in America, has a car, and dependence upon declining public transport may decrease mobility for certain groups. Apart from this there may, in the future, develop a countervailing trend in favour of reduced geographical mobility generally. Telecommunications make it possible to substitute movement of information for movement of people. 'Traditionally, we have moved the body to the experience; increasingly we will move the experience to the body, and the body can therefore be located where it finds the non-electronic experiences most satisfying' (Berry 1970 p 49). The development of telecommunications is still in the fairly early stages but the possibilities are already clear and are discussed in Units 18 and 30, and in the extract from Whyte in the Reader. Already it is possible to reduce the work force engaged on manual and clerical routines. The automatic transmission of data and the face-to-face communication via television may well substitute for movement of employees. Increasingly it will be possible for people to work, or be educated, at home. It is conceivable that in future there will be a dispersed, largely immobile work force, organized and interconnected by telecommunications. This may bring about a vast reduction in the journey-to-work flows, and in the demand for work space at accessible central locations. The increase in productivity and the savings in travel time that should result from better methods of communication, will be a major factor in the increase of leisure time predicted in Unit 30 and discussed by Tillinghast in the Reader.

It is difficult to be clear as to how far this trend may go, and what implications it has for social life. Leicester (1970) and Hall (1969) both portray urban life in the year 2000. The life of the Dumills is the ultimate expression of the mobile society. They live in a Kentish new town and travel long distances to work and for leisure. Their way of life is not vastly different from that of many people today though their spatial horizons are rather wider. Everybrit, by contrast, lives in a synthetic world where work routines are largely automatic with little scope for personal initiative. He has ample leisure time and, apparently, an abundance of ways in which to spend it. His world is, perhaps, similar to Huxley's *Brave New World* (see Reader extract) where technology has provided material well being at the expense of a regulated, stereotyped, conformist way of life. But in both examples people still feel the need for face-to-face interaction and travel remains a desirable experience. The ultimate horror of the immobile society in which each individual is incarcerated in an underground cell engaged in constant, yet trivial and meaningless intercourse

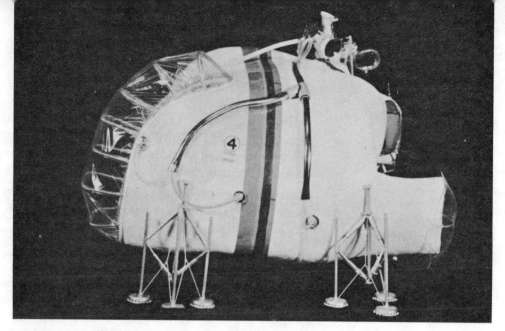

Figure 2 'Living Pod' by David Greene who describes it as a 'residential unit with integrated energy production and waste disposal systems'. It realizes Le Corbusier's concept of a 'machine to live in' and demonstrates that the cellular city foreshadowed by Forster in *The Machine Stops* is technologically practicable Source: Archigram Architects

through the Machine is vividly outlined in *The machine stops* (Forster in Reader). It is a portent not merely of the demise of the city but of the end of civilization itself.

SAQ 2 What evidence is there to suggest the eventual demise of the city as a spatial form?

SAQ 3 What evidence is there to suggest the continuation of the city as a spatial form?

2.2 Increasing social scale

The idea that the city may, at least in some areas and at some future time, cease to be an identifiable physical entity is relatively easy to understand. But the notion that the scale of urban society is increasing and is losing its separate identity is much more difficult to grasp. The explanation for the changing scale lies in the cumulative and all embracing process of industrialization and its accompanying characteristics – the decline of the agricultural labour force, increasing specialization and productivity, higher incomes, better education and so on. Society becomes organized in urban centres. A consequence of this is the transition from 'Gemeinschaft', to 'Gesellschaft', from a social organization centred on the family and the close-knit localized community towards one in which people participate in a wider world to which they are linked through their work, leisure interests and the mass media.[1] As the process continues so the larger scale society that develops in the city encroaches more and more on the small scale communities, whether rural or urban, until they are absorbed into it. At this stage urban society becomes subsumed by society itself.

Some commentators have, erroneously I feel, interpreted the changing structure of society as a decline in community. Stein in his book *The Eclipse of Community*, traces this decline in terms of the increasing scale of society brought about by the three interdependent processes of urbanization, industrialization and bureaucratization (Stein 1960). Thus, the very processes that are bringing about the demise of the city have according to Stein already been responsible for the eclipse of community. Stein, like Webber (who is basically concerned with the spatial rather than the sociological changes in community structure), identifies an increasing dispersal of activities. He goes further and delivers a vituperative attack on the suburban values that have

---

[1] *Gemeinschaft* and *Gesellschaft* are defined in Unit 6, page 20 and discussed in Unit 7, page 54.

replaced community. 'Large-scale organization creates small-scale personalities and meaningless jobs are filled by eager job holders' (Stein 1960 p 296). In this he betrays his own value orientation which equates community solely with a close-knit, local, social system.

The reality is more complex for communities may have both spatial and social connotations. The distinction was discussed in Unit 8, Section 3. Here we are concerned with the consequences of the distinction.

... The most important distinction is that between exclusive *membership* groups and inclusive *spatial* groups. Exclusive membership groups range in size from giant corporations to friendship cliques, and their tasks vary in comparable fashion; inclusive groups may be as small as neighbourhood, as large as London, with a comparable variation in size and complexity. The major difference is that the tasks of the exclusive membership groups have no necessary, inescapable base in a specific area; those of the inclusive spatial groups are all generated by the condition of its defining area. (Greer 1962 p 37)[1]

An interesting point brought out here is that communities whether of place or of interest exist at a variety of scales from the small (eg friendship cliques, neighbourhoods) to the large (business corporations, London). What appears to be happening is that through increasing societal scale the membership community has assumed many of the roles, norms, and activities of the spatial group.

... Commitment to place has weakened and people have become more nomadic, shifting from place-related social structures (city, state, nation or neighbourhood) to those (corporation, profession, friendship, network) that are themselves mobile, fluid, and for all practical purposes, place-less. (Toffler 1970)

This restive, compulsive mobility of the emerging urban society finds its spatial expression in the expansive, ubiquitous and abundant vision of Frank Lloyd Wright's *Broadacre City* (see excerpt in Reader).

In social terms the outlook is, according to some commentators, a gloomy one. In a situation of increasing scale it appears that large organizations come to dominate society and the individual more and more. Society is manipulated to achieve the goals of the state or the corporation.

The consequences of this kind of trend are spelled out in the extract from *A blueprint for survival* (Reader). The divorce between the goals of society and the needs of the individual grow until any relationship between them is lost. Then 'such a society will be characterized by a general feeling of aimlessness, a frantic, almost pathetic search for originality, over preoccupation with anything capable of providing short-term entertainment, and beneath it all a feeling of hopelessness of the futility of all effort' (Ecologist 1972).

This state is foreshadowed in the writings of Huxley and Forster, both of whom divine the most pessimistic consequences of increasing scale. In their world man has surrendered his control over the environment to the technology he has created. The physically fragile, feeble-minded cell-bound inmate of Forster's underground city is the ultimate doom of man, the antithesis of the gregarious, satisfied beings that inhabit Plato's *Republic* or More's *Utopia*. Curiously there are parallels between the organization of these joyless dystopias and the (apparently) serene world of the utopians. Both are highly stratified societies

1 Exclusive membership groups are similar to Webber's 'communities of interest' and, likewise, his 'communities of place' may be related to inclusive spatial groups. We are here concerned more with the social than the spatial manifestations of increasing scale.

Figure 3 Max Ernst, 'The Petrified City', 1933 Source: City Art Gallery, Manchester

where communal social controls are pervasive and have usurped those exercised by the family. Both are ruled by a benevolent paternalistic elite (the Philosopher-Rulers of Plato, the Syphogrants of More, Mustapha Mond in Huxley). It is in their goals that they are so markedly different. The constraints imposed on utopians are necessary if society is to be completely ordered. The coercion applied in the dystopias is essential to prevent the assertion of individual independence, and education takes the form of a repetitive brainwashing that stifles antisocial thought. As Huxley puts it in his Foreword to the 1950 edition of *Brave New World*, 'the problems of such societies will be "the problem of happiness" – in other words, the problem of making people love their servitude' (p xiv).

SAQ 4 What is meant by increasing social scale?

SAQ 5 What process is responsible for increasing social scale?

SAQ 6 Does an increase in social scale threaten the existence of spatially defined communities?

SAQ 7 What effect is an increase of scale likely to have on the city?

SAQ 8 What significance may increasing social scale have on the future of society?

2.3 The future of small scale communities

The portrait of a global society dominated by a complex and irresistible technology in which man is physically impotent and psychologically cowed is a commonplace of futuristic writing. But it is only an interpretation of the possible outcome of current trends, a warning rather than a prediction. An alternative to this, and one constantly stressed in two of the excerpts in the

Figure 4 Popular demonstration Source: The Guardian

Reader (the Ecologist, and Ward and Dubos) is a return to a smaller, a more human scale.

Man's need for the small scale, for an intimate face-to-face frame of reference is, apparently, innate and essential:

... a community in which different families and individuals can meet and get to know each other face-to-face, band together for common enterprises, support each other against outside interventions and experience a sense of the more profound significance of their daily living has been seen to be a need among living creatures ever since man emerged from the primal groups of herd and pack. (Ward and Dubos 1972 p 146)

The Greek city-state was small enough for a form of direct democracy to flourish. In Athens the vote was restricted to adult males (thus excluding women, children, slaves, and the foreign born) who numbered about 45,000–50,000 but 'within this body of voting citizens popular control was complete'. (Introduction to Lee's translation of Plato's *Republic* 1955 p 22). Although the form of government was criticized for its inefficiency,[1] the remarkable fact was that, for a time, it existed. In modern society we hear much of the need for more individual viewpoints to be articulated in order to meet a variety of needs. This has led to the development of advocacy planning as practised in America (Unit 22 and Davidoff 1968 in Reader), and to neighbourhood councils in Britain. Occasionally, even in these countries popular demonstrations of local feeling are aroused against specific grievances (Figure 4). Existing administrative structures appear unable to deal with many of the problems experienced at the individual or small group level.

1 Plato, for example, said: 'It's an agreeable, anarchic form of society, with plenty of variety, which treats all men as equal, whether they be equal or not' (*The Republic* pp 330–1).

These arguments for decentralization and the creation of small communities tend to present a rather one-sided viewpoint as is suggested in Unit 30 (see especially Sections 5.3.4 and 5.3.5). They infer that the size of cities is a determinant of social malaise rather than a dependent variable of social organization. It is, in any case, open to question whether a man or woman can only be an individual in a small community. Certainly, an individual is known in most if not all his roles in the village community, whereas in the city he is normally seen in different roles by different people. It is arguable whether this makes him more of an individual, however. In many instances it may inhibit him out of a fear of social disapproval. The impersonality and anonymity of the city are not wholly negative as is often made out. They may offer a great deal in the way of freedom for the individual. He is not constrained by a small social group. He can pick and choose as he wishes from the multiplicity of subgroups within the city, creating for himself the life style he desires. This is not to dispute the loneliness and isolation that can exist in cities, but they may exist in small communities too.

SAQ 9 Does the growth of the city inhibit the development of small scale communities?

2.4 Summary In the advanced industrial countries it can be argued that cities have grown so large and their institutions so specialized and remote that they can no longer cope effectively with small scale problems. As cities assume more and more the characteristics of mass society they begin to surrender their independence as a concept with which people can identify. When this happens do people inevitably shift their allegiance to the dispersed communities of interest that are the outcome of increasing mobility as predicted by Webber and Toffler?

Figure 5 Park Hill Development, Sheffield, 1961 Comprehensive redevelopment of the inner city provides a physical expression of the increasing scale that may characterize the future city Source: Aerofilms Ltd

Or will there be a return to the small scale, face-to-face, and localized community as advocated by others? (see, especially, excerpt from *The Ecologist* in Reader). The answer may be both.

The two types of community are not mutually exclusive but are interrelated and interdependent within the total social system. Members of an inclusive locality group can also belong to exclusive communities of interest. These latter may possess some territoriality. 'The local setting of the organization has a strong tendency to foster local commitments' (Greer 1962 p 53). Looked at in this way communities of various size composed of people related through interlocking networks are found to coexist within a given area. Therefore by adopting either a specifically spatial or specifically social perspective we may neglect the interaction between them.

SAQ 10 What kind of communities may be typical in the future?

3 The role of the city in society

From the previous discussion it might be inferred that by focusing on the city we have chosen a specific and thereby limiting perspective. This might lead us to ignore what remains of the non-urban (very little in advanced societies but the greater part of the developing world) and to overlook the components which make up the city. In fact this course has tended to limit itself to studying the city as a social and spatial entity. We have looked at the subsystems (social, economic, technological, and political) that operate within the urban system; and we have analysed levels of organization (eg the neighbourhood, the central business district) that compose elements of these subsystems; and in this unit I have tried to relate the urban system to the society of which it is an integral part.

The city remains as not merely a dominant settlement form, but as the control centre of society. The major cities house the headquarters of the major corporations, they are the seats of national and regional administration, from them are diffused information and innovations; and to them people look for their cultural and social needs. For many the city is the centre of power, the creator of wealth, and the symbol of culture. It represents a heavy investment of social and economic capital that could only be replaced at enormous cost. Rather than dwindle or collapse, the city may become, and in many parts of the world is, 'the normal human habitat' (Lynch 1961 p 82). This view of the city as a thriving, dynamic entity is in apparent contradistinction to that emphasized in this unit so far.

The view that is held of the future of the city depends on how the evidence is interpreted. Those who hold that the city will become increasingly diffused spatially and lose its identity as a form of social organization point to the changing scale of society. Larger scale (ie national and international) and smaller scale forms of social organization present more relevant centres of attention. On the other hand there are those who believe the process of urban diffusion and its social connotations is culturally specific, confined to the USA and the western and south western USA at that. It is a phenomenon that emanates from areas that have never had an urban tradition as experienced in eastern USA or Europe. They argue that to attribute to the process universal inevitability grossly neglects the permanence of existing settlement forms and social structures and the strength of cultural values. It is a process that is totally irrelevant to the situation in the inner areas of many western cities or in the developing world where conditions of affluence and mobility have yet to be experienced.

4 The relevance of the city to the problems of society

So far the demise of the city has been considered in an academic sense. The question of the city as a relevant focus of study may be posed in a rather more practical way. Does the study of urban development help us to identify urban problems which require political solutions? The evidence of the course seems to suggest that it does. Among the urban problems referred to are those that affect the efficient organization of functions within the city such as the distribution of services and industry (Block 3), the role of public transport, or the disposal of urban wastes and effluent (Block 4). There are also those problems that relate to the overall planning and administration of the city (Blocks 5 and 7). Problems such as these may be classed as urban in the sense that they originate within a defined urban space. But, they may affect non-urban areas (eg waste disposal, exurban growth) and require subsidy from national funds if they are to be successfully tackled.

Study of particular urban problems may lead you to consider the distribution of opportunities whether in transport, housing, employment, education, or amenity. Some groups clearly benefit from living in cities, others do not. This question of the relative deprivation of specific social groups has been an implicit theme throughout the course. It is evident in the enormous contrast in living standards and aspirations between the developing and the advanced countries. It is significant also in the gulf between rich and poor that exists within all countries. In the developing world deprivation affects a majority of the urban population. In the advanced countries the 'urban problem' expressed in contrasts of income and environment is largely confined to the inner city areas:

... The cities ... took the brunt of the contrasts – in the pockets of poverty in slum and ghetto in developed lands, in the shanty towns and favellas, the calampas and bidonvilles which began to surround developing cities with the squalid camps and shelters of millions of immigrants from rural misery'. (Ward and Dubos 1972 p 61)

Poverty is a social, not an urban problem, though some of its worst manifestations may be found in the cities. Although in advanced societies, especially, the operation of social processes has tended to concentrate poverty in the cities we should not be misled into thinking that the problem can be defined and its solution provided for in an urban context alone (see Webber in Bourne 1971). Davidoff (1968) in the Reader makes the point:

... The concern with urbanism is misplaced. The real crisis of our times is not an urban crisis. Instead, the crucial problem is a national problem, an international problem, a social problem. It is the fact of great social injustice'. (Davidoff 1968)

Cities are quite unable to provide, within their own resources, for the amelioration of the disproportionate amount of material and social deprivation that exists within them. The position is often exacerbated by the fact that, unless boundary reforms keep pace with urban spread, cities are tending (in western societies) to lose the more affluent members of their population who may nevertheless still place burdens upon the facilities and transport of the central city. Aside from the resource aspect, social and economic inequality is a feature of society as a whole and not merely of the urban (or rural) part of it.

Inequality may be economic in the sense of the maldistribution of wealth and opportunities; political in that power is unevenly divided; and social in that some cultural traits (race, religion or language) may lead to differences of status. There is often a correlation of these characteristics among certain groups living in certain areas. From basic inequalities stem many of the conflicts and tensions that beset societies. Since they occur at all levels in society the city is not the appropriate theatre in which to devise solutions. In so far as concern with the urban aspect of social problems diverts attention from the causes of these problems, study of the city *per se* may be an obstacle to the application of appropriate solutions.

SAQ 11   To what extent can social problems be solved or ameliorated within the context of the city?

5 The demise of society?

Questions of social justice or economic growth relate urban development to the wider issue of the development of society as a whole. We become aware of the urban system as a part of the complex global system that incorporates the interactions of man with his environment. A feature of systems is that they tend to grow exponentially. The intimate interdependence of the components that comprise the biosphere has been a recurrent theme of philosophical and scientific writing. It has recently acquired a more urgent tone as the grim and immediate prospects of exponential population and economic growth have been emphasized by certain commentators (The Ecologist 1972, Ward and Dubos 1972, and Meadows *et al* 1972). They hold that the delicate dynamic equilibrium of nature is likely to be seriously disturbed. For example increased pollution is reducing the abundance of life in some rivers. Monocultural practices and pesticides and fertilisers may, ultimately, combine to reduce soil fertility. Industrial development is bringing about the depletion of natural resources. The essential complexity upon which the stability of ecosystems depends has become disturbed.

On present trends world population will have doubled to around 7,000 million by 2000, many non-renewable resources will be nearing exhaustion, and pollution will have massively increased. These depressing forecasts are based on the extrapolation of current trends; a technique we examined critically in Unit 30. According to the logic of exponential growth the stage has already been reached when the *doubling time* of world population is a generation or so.

Figure 6 Exponential growth 'Doubling time' is the time it takes for a growing quantity to double in size. This is roughly equal to 70 divided by the growth rate and the table gives examples of the doubling times at different growth rates. The graph compares linear growth (a set increase in a particular period) and exponential growth (a percentage increase in a particular period) of investment illustrating the principle of 'doubling time'. Source: Meadows *et al* (1972) Figure 4

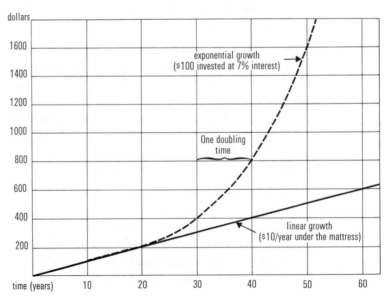

If a miser hides $10 each year under his mattress, his savings will grow linearly, as shown by the lower curve. If, after 10 years, he invests his $100 at 7 per cent interest, that $100 will grow exponentially, with a doubling time of 10 years.

Table 1 Exponential growth

Growth rate (% per year)	Doubling time (years)
0.1	700
0.5	140
1.0	70
2.0	35
4.0	18
5.0	14
7.0	10
10.0	7

Source: Meadows *et al* (1972) Table 1

Exponential growth occurs when a quantity increases by a given percentage in given time period. It is quite different from *linear growth* which occurs when a quantity increases by a given amount in a given time period. Thus a population that increased by one million per year would be experiencing linear growth, whereas one growing by two per cent per year would be growing exponentially. It would take this latter population thirty-five years to double its size (*doubling time*).

A characteristic of exponential growth is that a given amount increases (or decreases) with accelerating speed. It is estimated, for example, that the 1970 resource base was still about ninety-five per cent of its 1900 value but that by 2000 with exponential growth in consumption it could be virtually exhausted. At present rates of consumption with existing known reserves and technology copper supplies would last thirty-six years but only twenty-one years if the present exponential growth rate is maintained.

Economic growth varies from country to country but even at two per cent per annum an economy can double its output within thirty-five years (see Figure 6 and Table 1). Resource depletion is even more rapid. Even if action were taken immediately to reduce population and economic growth the existing momentum would make it impossible to achieve stability until well into the next century. Unless restraint is exercised the forecasters predict the 'collapse of society':

... This is the hinge of history at which we stand, the door of the future opening on to a crisis more sudden, more global, more inescapable, and more bewildering than any ever encountered by the human species ... (Ward and Dubos 1972 p 47)

The forms the collapse will take – worldwide famine, intolerable pollution, or self-destruction through a global Armageddon – represent a choice of unpleasant and equally final alternatives.

Such a future is possible if present trends continue inexorably. But it is not inevitable although predictions based on extrapolated trends tend to give an illusion of inevitability. In fact, any continuation of existing trends over a long period is highly unlikely and we should treat such forecasts with circumspection (see Jencks in Reader). Take the question of resources for example. Predictions of a world shortage of oil are based on the fact that the growth in production has recently exceeded the growth in reserves. Conversely, in the early 1960s when the growth of reserves outpaced the growth in production there was general optimism about the future of oil.

Global forecasts of this type often fail to reveal the underlying assumptions. In the case of oil, reserves are calculated on the basis of 'proved' reserves, ie those that can be economically exploited in the prevailing constraints of technology and price. What happens if these constraints change and a calculation is made for reserves which new methods of exploitation and higher recovery rates would render viable? Resources that are at present uneconomic, such as the oil shales and tar sands of North America, may be exploited if prices rise in the future. Recent oil price increases have tended to reflect the higher royalties paid to producing states rather than any increases in the costs of production. If prices rise above those of competitive fuels then some substitution may be expected. In the future as more expensive reserves have to be used, oil may be displaced from its dominant position in the world energy market. Darmstadter is persuaded that world energy resources are quite sufficient.

... No matter whether one focuses on lower or upper limits of estimated *total* fossil fuel resources (coal, oil, gas), the picture that emerges is one of vast quantities implying world wide abundance of energy sources far into the distant future (Darmstadter *et al* 1971 p 50)

This is, of course, an opinion but it is one to set against that of those forecasting imminent exhaustion of certain supplies.

In the case of tin, the extrapolated forecasts suggest exhaustion of reserves at exponential rates of consumption within about fifteen years (Meadows *et al* 1972 Table 4 p 56). Any figure given for tin reserves is notional. Although some attempts have been made at accurate estimation (eg Robertson 1964) the definition of reserves in terms of accessibility and quality varies and large areas have not been fully surveyed. The future of the metal is much more dependent on price and the state of technology. Since a control scheme is operated to contain price fluctuations it is difficult to relate production costs to prices. The price support arising from control may have encouraged the use of substitutes for tin. More important has been the introduction of new tinning processes which have reduced the weight of tin in tinplate, its major market.

Although there is a finite limit to natural resources it is impossible to predict with any certainty when they will become exhausted. More efficient usage, recycling, and substitution will alter the situation in the future as they have in the past. Similarly, the other predictions based on exponential growth rates may have similar mechanisms of change. Thus population growth could slow down towards zero growth as it appears to be doing in western Europe at the present time. Increasing concern at the rising level of pollution might encourage rigorous preventive measures. Reduction in the exponential growth of population, pollution, and capital formation could lead to a situation of equilibrium, the stable society advocated by the environmentalists. The resource base would no longer be threatened and there would be sufficient food for every individual.

Under conditions of stability technology would be directed towards resource conservation through improving durability and reducing waste, and society as a whole might lean towards the provision of education and leisure rather than towards increasing the means of industrial production and consumption. Freed from concentrating on material prosperity, other goals will occupy the energies of man. The objectives of social equality and justice are 'far more likely to evolve in a state of global equilibrium than ... in the state of growth we are experiencing today' (Meadows *et al* 1972 p 175). As a result 'the important issue of the stationary state will be distribution, not production' (Meadows *et al* 1972 p 175). In putting this case the environmentalists are deliberately departing from the conventional economic wisdom which assumes it is easier to achieve the social goals of a distributional nature in a growing economy.

It is no coincidence that this shift in emphasis and in the fundamental values of society would produce a situation similar in certain respects to that outlined by the utopians. In utopia production is only a means to an end and the goal of society is justice (Plato), or equality (More), and in both this is to be obtained through communal effort. Similarly, those who assert the need for change in the values of modern society place great emphasis on international cooperation in order to secure stability and social justice.

All this may seem a long way from the problem of urban development. The city is the result of the economic specialization that is the mainspring of growth. It is not an independent entity but part of a global system. For, all of us whether we live in what are called cities or not 'belong to a single system, powered by a single energy, manifesting a fundamental unity under all its variations' (Ward and Dubos 1972 p 297). If society as a whole must change then the city, too, must change. If the emphasis in the future is to be on the small scale, the community in which democracy can flourish, and in which the individual can effectively participate then the city as a large scale expression of economic power and specialization may be doomed. On an international scale the major issue will be the maintenance of stability, a function that even the major city will be too small to perform, or as the Ecologist believes, too big. If such a stable society is ever attained then the functions now performed by the city will have been absorbed by new institutions. Then, the demise of the city will have occurred.

SAQ 12   Why is the demise of society likely if present world trends continue?

SAQ 13   What factors are neglected by those who predict the imminent demise of society?

SAQ 14   What conditions are necessary for a stable society?

SAQ 15   What advantages might accrue to society under conditions of global equilibrium?

Comments on SAQs

Comment SAQ 1   Perhaps the most distinguishing feature of cities in the western USA is a physical one: the absence of contrast between urban and rural. The urban forms were largely created in the motor age and cities have dispersed at low densities across large territories. In other parts of the USA and in Europe, cities preceded the motor age and although they have, to some extent, adapted to it they still retain the compact, centralized form focused around the CBD and with densities declining outwards from it.

In a social sense there are less obvious distinguishing characteristics. Some (eg Webber, Davie, Toffler) would claim that mobility and affluence have proceeded so far in western USA that a distinctive culture unrelated to the city is emerging. It is, of course, a matter for speculation whether this trend will diffuse elsewhere and penetrate all social levels.

Comment SAQ 2 The evidence comes mainly from the USA. The idea that the spatial scale of urban form is changing there is commonplace. Some (eg Friedman and Miller) believe that urban function rather than form is characteristic of the urbanization process. Others, like Berry, consider the characteristic process is no longer specifically urban for innovations may occur in areas remote from cities. The car has enabled cities to spread and telecommunications may in the future eliminate the significance of distance, if not (as Forster warns) the need for movement. At that stage the conventional idea of urban form will be irrelevant.

Comment SAQ 3 In the USA Wolf considers urban forms are changing but not disappearing. The process of outward spread has increased the size of cities but they remain distinctive entities. In Britain, planning controls have maintained a fairly clear physical delimitation between town and country although the divide is not so clear cut in a social sense.

Comment SAQ 4 The idea of social scale is a difficult one to comprehend. A change in social scale implies a transfer of focus from small scale to large scale forms of organization. Examples of small scale organizations are the family, neighbourhood, village and large scale organizations include business corporations, the city and the state. The transfer from *Gemeinschaft* to *Gesellschaft* discussed in Units 6 and 7 is obviously related to changes in social scale.

Comment SAQ 5 The process could broadly be described as industrialization and the related processes of urbanization and bureaucratization. This has resulted in changes in occupational structure (eg a shift from primary to manufacturing and service industries), and family status (eg smaller families, higher incomes, better education, more women at work). As a result individuals participate in a much wider society.

Comment SAQ 6 An increase in social scale can encourage participation in communities of interest as well as those that are place related. In general, it does appear that exclusive groups based on particular interests have become more significant than inclusive groups that are locality based (but see also SAQ 10).

Comment SAQ 7 In certain ways the city is itself a product of increasing social scale. Though it is a community of place it also fosters communities of interest. As these increase in significance the social relevance of place communities, including the city, may well diminish further.

Comment SAQ 8 It is arguable that increasing social scale will lead to the dominance of large organizations. Society will then become rigidly stratified and totalitarian. This view reflects the part that small scale organizations may play in instigating the trend towards centralization.

Comment SAQ 9 It is sometimes difficult for small scale locality based communities to find expression or articulate their needs in the framework of urban organization. But the city may encourage rather than inhibit the freedom of expression of individuals.

Comment SAQ 10   It has been suggested that large scale communities, whether inclusive or exclusive are supplanting small scale ones. *The Ecologist* makes the point, however, that small scale communities may be essential to survival. In the future it is quite likely that communities of all types – inclusive or exclusive, large or small – will coexist and that individuals may belong to several at any one time. The variety is likely to increase.

Comment SAQ 11   Social problems cannot be solved within the context of the city for two reasons. First, cities tend to have a disproportionate share of social problems and must also provide facilities for a surrounding population. They rarely command the resources themselves to cope with all the demands made upon them and must depend to some extent on central funds. Second, although social problems are concentrated in the city they are manifestations of basic inequalities of income and class which can only be solved at a societal level.

Comment SAQ 12   According to many observers exponential growth is characteristic of the global ecosystem. The limits to growth of that system are applied by the availability of land and natural resources and the capacity of the biosphere to absorb pollution. If population, resource depletion and pollution continue to grow at an accelerating rate then the limits to growth will be reached within a relatively short period, perhaps a generation or so.

Comment SAQ 13   The prediction is based on the assumption that present growth rates will be experienced in the future. Although the logic of exponential growth is irrefutable there are few grounds for assuming that exponential growth will continue indefinitely (see Unit 30, Section 3). Moreover, the possibility of substitution is neglected in the extrapolation of existing trends. It is possible that some resources may be substituted by capital or alternative resources. Higher recovery rates or greater productivity may reduce resource depletion. The current trends in population growth, pollution or food production are all subject to considerable change.

Comment SAQ 14   The stable society represents a situation where each component of the global system is in dynamic equilibrium. Thus, the number of births would be counterbalanced by the number of deaths giving a stable population. The growth in investment would be the same as the amount of depreciation giving a stable capital stock (meaning services, industry, and agricultural capital combined).

Comment SAQ 15   Environmentalists argue that in a stable society the competitive pressures that engender conflict and inequality would be eliminated. Instead, society could set new goals such as increasing social justice which it could seek to achieve through a fundamental redistribution of wealth at a global level. This implies a shift in social values. It is quite different from the conventional argument that redistribution can best be effected under conditions of economic growth.

References   BALLARD, J. G. (1966) *Billennium*, in KNIGHT, D. (ed) *Cities of Wonder*, Sphere Books edition 1970.

BERRY, B. J. L. (1970) 'The Geography of the United States in the year 2000' in *Transactions, Institute of British Geographers*, 51.

BOURNE, L. S. (ed) (1971) *Internal Structure of the City*, New York, Oxford University Press (set book).

DARMSTADTER, J. *et al* (1971) *Energy in the world economy*, Resources for the future.

DAVIE, M. (1972) 'The end of the city' in *In the future now*, London, Hamish Hamilton, pp 72–92 (in the Reader).

DAVIDOFF, P. (1968) 'Normative planning' in ANDERSON, S. (ed) (1968) *Planning for diversity and choice*, Cambridge, Mass., MIT Press.

ECOLOGIST (1972) *A blueprint for survival*, Harmondsworth, Penguin Books (originally published in *The Ecologist*, 2, 1, 1972).

FORSTER, E. M. (1928) 'The machine stops' in *The eternal moment and other stories*, London, Sidgwick and Jackson.

FRIEDMAN, J. and MILLER, J. (1965) 'The urban field' in *Journal of American Institute of Planners*, 31, pp 312–9.

GREER, S. (1962) *The emerging city, myth and reality*, New York, The Free Press.

HALL, P. (1969) *London 2000*, London, Faber and Faber (paperback 1971).

HUXLEY, A. (1967) *Brave New World*, London, Chatto and Windus.

KELLER, SUZANNE (1972) 'Beyond the city: need for a city' in *American Behavioral Scientist*, 15, pp 591–605.

LYNCH, K. (1961) 'The pattern of the metropolis' in *Daedalus*, Winter, pp 79–98.

LEICESTER, C. (1970) 'Life in the year 2000 AD' in MACARTHUR, B. (ed) (1970) *New horizons for education*, London, Council for Educational Advance.

MEADOWS, DONELLA H., MEADOWS, D. L., RONDERS, J. and BEHRENS, W. W. III (1972) *The limits to growth*, London, Earth Island.

ROBERTSON, W. (1964) *Report on the world tin position*, London, International Tin Council.

SIMAK, CLIFFORD (1952) *City*, Weidenfeld and Nicolson (Science Fiction Book Club (1961).

STEIN, M. R. (1960) *The Eclipse of Community*, New York, Harper and Row.

TILLINGHAST, P. (1968) 'Leisure' in ANDERSON, S. (ed) (1968) *Planning for diversity and choice*, Cambridge, Mass., MIT Press.

TOFFLER, A. (1970) *Future shock*, London, Bodley Head; also Pan Books 1973.

WARD, BARBARA and DUBOS, RENÉE (1972) *Only one earth*, Harmondsworth, Penguin Books.

WEBBER, M. M. (1963) 'Order in diversity; Community without propinquity' in WINGO, L. JR. (ed) (1963) *Cities and space*, Baltimore, Johns Hopkins Press (paperback 1966).

WEBER, M. (1958) *The City*, New York, The Free Press.

WOLF, L. G. (1969) 'The metropolitan tidal wave in Ohio' in *Economic Geography*, 45, pp 133–54.

WRIGHT, F. L. (1932) 'City of the future must be based on the new scale of spacing' in *The disappearing city*, New York, W. F. Payson.

Acknowledgements   Grateful acknowledgement is made for material used in this unit:

Figure 1: USIS; *Figure 2*: Archigram Architects; *Figure 3*: SPADEM; *Figure 4*: Guardian Newspapers Ltd; *Figure 5*: Aerofilms Ltd; *Figure 6 and Table 1*: in Donella H. Meadows, et al *The Limits to Growth*, Earth Island Publishers, London, 1972.

Urban development